W9-DAY-588

DATE DUE

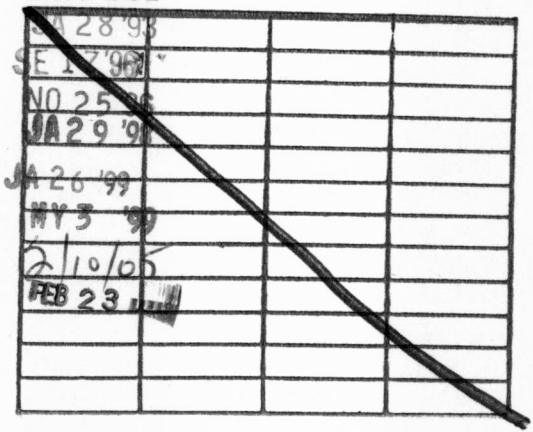

DEMCO

After the People Vote

After the People Vote

A Guide to the Electoral College

Revised and Enlarged Edition

Edited by Walter Berns

With Essays by
Norman J. Ornstein and Martin Diamond

The AEI Press

Publisher for the American Enterprise Institute
WASHINGTON, D.C.

1992

Distributed by arrangement with

University Press of America
4720 Boston Way   3 Henrietta Street
Lanham, Md. 20706   London WC2E 8LU England

Library of Congress Cataloging-in-Publication Data

After the people vote : a guide to the electoral college / edited
  by Walter Berns ; with essays by Norman J. Ornstein and
  Martin Diamond.—2nd ed.
        p.   cm.—(AEI studies ; 542)
     ISBN 0-8447-3803-4—ISBN 0-8447-3802-6 (pbk.)
       1. Presidents—United States—Election.   I. Berns,
     Walter, 1919–   . II. Ornstein, Norman J.   III. Diamond,
     Martin, 1919–   . IV. Series.
     JK529.A68   1992   91-32732
     324.6'0973—dc20   CIP

1   3   5   7   9   10   8   6   4   2

AEI Studies 542

The AEI Press
Publisher for the American Enterprise Institute
1150 Seventeenth Street, N.W., Washington, D.C. 20036

Printed in the United States of America

Contents

Preface

It is always possible that an independent candidate for the presidency will deprive one of the major party candidates of an electoral college majority. In 1980, when the pre-election polls showed the independent John Anderson to have substantial popular support, this possibility gave rise to a number of articles purporting to describe what might happen "if nobody wins." Some of these were highly imaginative, and none of them, sober or imaginative, was accurate in all its details. For example, in an *Atlantic Monthly* piece the constitutional lawyer Laurence H. Tribe and Thomas M. Rollins suggested that Congress might appoint a commission to resolve electoral disputes, as it did in 1876. That commission was appointed to determine which electors from several disputed states should be allowed to vote. In 1887, however, Congress passed a law, still in force, to prevent a recurrence of what had happened in 1876. The procedure for choosing a president when no candidate has a majority of electoral votes is discussed in chapter 5, and an account of the 1876 election and two other disputed elections in chapter 9.

Because of mistakes of this sort and the unavailability of an authoritative document on presidential selection, several of us political scientists associated with the American Enterprise Institute decided to prepare this guide for students, for the press, and for the general public. Because the system involves interactions between the Constitution, federal and state statutes, and party and parliamentary rules, this study should be useful to all those interested in the American political system.

The original edition of this guide was "keyed" to the election of 1984. Thus, for example, the date given for the appointment of electors—election day, as we know it popularly—was November 6, and the date given for electors to meet in their various capitals and cast their votes for president and vice president was December 17. But the federal statute fixing these times speaks not of November 6 and December 17 but of "the Tuesday next after the first Monday in November," and "the first Monday after the second Wednesday in December next following their appointment," and the dates corresponding to these times will, of course, vary with the calendar. Accordingly, in each case we have, in this edition, given the dates for the election years 1992, 1996, and 2000, after which—since there will then have been another decennial census, and with it a reallocation of electoral votes among the states (see appendix F)—still another edition of this guide will be necessary.

The provisions appearing in the appendixes are those in force in 1991, but changes might, of course, be made. Congress might amend the statutory provisions governing the electoral process (see appendix B), and before the year 2000 at least some of the states are likely to change their provisions respecting the nomination and binding of electors (see appendix C). The Democratic and Republican parties may even change their rules dealing with the death or resignation of presidential and vice presidential candidates (see appendix E). Fortunately (for those of us who prepared this guide and, we think, for the country), the constitutional provisions (see appendix A) are not so readily changed.

The following persons contributed to this second edition or offered their counsel: Robert Goldwin, Michael Malbin, Thomas Mann, Norman Ornstein, Howard Penniman, Austin Ranney, and Richard M. Scammon. They were assisted by Anne R. Dias.

WALTER BERNS
Washington, D.C.

Contributors

WALTER BERNS is John M. Olin University Professor at Georgetown University and adjunct scholar at the American Enterprise Institute. He has also taught at the University of Toronto and Cornell and Yale universities. His government service includes membership on the National Council on the Humanities, the Council of Scholars in the Library of Congress, and the Judicial Fellows Commission, and in 1983 he was the alternate United States representative to the United Nations Commission on Human Rights. He has been a Guggenheim, Rockefeller, and Fulbright fellow and a Phi Beta Kappa lecturer. He is the author of numerous articles on American government in both professional and popular journals; his books include *In Defense of Liberal Democracy* and *Taking the Constitution Seriously*.

MARTIN DIAMOND died in 1977 just before he was to assume the Leavey Chair on the Foundations of American Freedom at Georgetown University.

He had taught at the University of Chicago, Illinois Institute of Technology, Claremont Men's College, Claremont Graduate School, and Northern Illinois University.

Diamond also served as a fellow of the Center for Advanced Study in the Behavioral Sciences, the Rockefeller Foundation, the Relm Foundation, the Woodrow Wilson International Center for Scholars, and the National Humanities Institute. A frequent adviser to private and public agencies and to state, local, and federal officials, including senators, congressmen, and presidents and vice presidents of the United States, he spent the last morning of his life testifying before a Senate committee on the electoral college.

His essays appear in *As Far as Republican Principles Will Admit: Essays by Martin Diamond* (AEI Press, 1992).

ROBERT A. GOLDWIN is resident scholar in constitutional studies at the American Enterprise Institute. He served in the White House as special consultant to the president of the United States and, concurrently, as adviser to the secretary of defense. He has taught at the University of Chicago and Kenyon College, and was dean of St. John's College in Annapolis, Maryland. He is the author of *Why Blacks, Women, and Jews Are Not Mentioned in the Constitution* and the editor or coeditor of more than a score of books including *How Democratic Is the Constitution?*, *How Does the Constitution Secure Rights?*, *Slavery and Its Consequences: the Constitution, Equality, and Race,* and *How Federal Is the Constitution?*.

MICHAEL J. MALBIN is professor of political science at the State University of New York at Albany and director of the Center for Legislature Studies at SUNY's Rockefeller Institute of Government. He is the author of *Money and Politics in the United States* and *Unelected Representatives,* and coauthor of the series *Vital Statistics on Congress,* and he has written numerous articles on American government. He was a resident fellow at the American Enterprise Institute from 1977 to 1986 and has held various positions in government service, among them minority staff member of the Iran-contra committee, associate director of the Office of the House Republican Conference, associate director of the Office of the House Republican whip, and speechwriter to the secretary of defense.

THOMAS E. MANN is director of governmental studies at the Brookings Institution. Formerly the executive director of the American Political Science Association and codirector of the Congress Project of the American Enterprise Institute, he is the author of *Unsafe at Any Margin: Interpreting Congressional Elections* and coauthor of *Vital Statistics on Congress.*

NORMAN J. ORNSTEIN is resident scholar at the American Enterprise Institute; political contributor to the MacNeil/ Lehrer NewsHour; election analyst for CBS News; and codirector of *The People, Press & Politics,* a Times Mirror Company study of the American electorate. He has also been a founding member, and member of the board of directors, of the National Commission on the Public Service, chaired by Paul Volcker. Ornstein is coauthor of the forthcoming *Debt and Taxes* and of the series *Vital Statistics on Congress* and editor of *The Role of Legislatures in Western Democracies, The New Congress,* and *Balancing Act.*

HOWARD PENNIMAN is adjunct scholar at the American Enterprise Institute and editor of its At the Polls series. He has been codirector of its program in political and social processes, an election consultant to the American Broadcasting Company, and a delegate to the Maryland Constitutional Convention. He taught at the University of Alabama, Yale University, and, for more than twenty years, Georgetown University. He has been an official election observer for the U.S. government in Vietnam, Rhodesia, Zimbabwe, El Salvador, Guatemala, and Taiwan.

AUSTIN RANNEY is professor emeritus of political science at the University of California, Berkeley. From 1976 to 1986 he was resident scholar at the American Enterprise Institute and is now adjunct scholar at AEI. He is the author or coauthor of books on American politics and parties, including *The Doctrine of Responsible Party Government, Democracy and the American Party System, Curing the Mischief of Factions,* and *Channels of Power: The Impact of Television on American Politics,* and editor of *The American Elections of*

1980 and *The American Elections of 1984.* He is former managing editor of *The American Political Science Review* and president of the American Political Science Association.

RICHARD M. SCAMMON is director of the Elections Research Center, editor of America at the Polls and of the America Votes series, and coauthor of *This U.S.A.* and *The Real Majority.* He served as a military government officer in Stuttgart and Berlin (1946–1948), as chief, Division of Research for Western Europe, U.S. Department of State (1948–1955), and as a member of the U.S. delegations observing elections in El Salvador, the Dominican Republic, Vietnam, the USSR, and the Gaza strip and the West Bank. For many years he was a senior elections consultant for NBC News and visiting fellow at the American Enterprise Institute. In 1961–1965 he was director of the U.S. Bureau of the Census.

PART ONE

How the Electoral College Works

Edited by Walter Berns

1

Introduction

The United States has avoided crises when a new president is elected in part because the electoral college exaggerates the margin of victory in the popular vote. This amplification gives us a clear winner even when the popular vote is close enough to be called a "photo-finish." Nevertheless, it is always possible that a third-party candidate, by winning a state or two, may prevent either of the major party candidates from winning the electoral college majority required by the Constitution. Recent changes in the law may well increase the number of third-party candidates. Court decisions have made ballot access easier, and the Federal Election Campaign Act ensures public funding, in advance of an election, for any minor party that received at least 5 percent of the vote in the previous presidential election.

Third parties have not fared well in America because, in part, the voting procedure of the electoral college deflates the strength of minor parties and inflates the margin of victory of the winning party. By state law, all electoral votes (except Maine's and Nebraska's) are awarded on a winner-take-all basis to the candidate who captures the most votes within that state. To have any electoral effect, then, a party must capture pluralities within states. A third party with an evenly spread national appeal, but lacking plurality support within any state, may find itself polling more than 20 percent of the popular vote without winning a single electoral vote. Millard Fillmore and the Know-Nothings polled 21 percent of the popular vote in 1856, but received only 2 percent of the electoral vote. William Howard Taft was the choice of 23 percent of the voters in 1912 but of only 1.5 percent of the electoral college.

Regional third-party challenges fare somewhat better in the electoral college, if only because they may win some states. In 1968, in the most successful third-party bid in a half-century, George Wallace captured forty-six electoral votes, but the electoral college still deflated his challenge. Although he had won 13.5 percent of the popular vote, he captured only 8 percent of the electoral vote; some 4.1 million Wallace votes outside the states he carried had been "wasted."

The electoral college's deflation of votes for a third party imposes a psychological burden on its campaigns: somehow, voters must be persuaded that they would not be throwing away their votes, while the two major parties—and the history of third-party efforts—insist that the voters would be doing just that. Even Wallace's full-scale national effort failed to overcome this burden. He watched his support fade from a high of 23 percent, in a September opinion survey, to an actual popular vote of 13.5 percent, at least in part because of the wasted vote argument.

Wallace's express purpose had been to win enough electoral votes in that very close race to block a majority for Richard Nixon or Hubert Humphrey in the electoral college. Then he planned to trade his electoral votes for policy concessions from one or the other of the major parties before the electoral college voted. It was feared, however, that the only result of his efforts would be to throw the election into the House of Representatives.

In any event the strategy of deadlocking the vote in the electoral college is a ticklish one. A third party not only must capture some states, but also must be careful elsewhere not to draw votes from only one of the two major candidates and give the other one a landslide. Because of the unit-rule method of awarding state votes, the winner of the plurality of the national popular vote usually receives an amplified majority of the electoral votes. For example, John Kennedy won only 49.7 percent of the popular vote in 1960, but he won 56.4 percent of the electoral votes, even though Harry F. Byrd won fifteen electoral votes (eight in Mississippi, six in Alabama, and one in Oklahoma).

This rule operates even when third-party challenges are strong and thus frustrates the strategy of throwing the election into the House. In the face of George Wallace's challenge in 1968, for example, Nixon received only 43.4 percent of the popular vote, but 55.9 percent of the electoral vote; and in 1980, when John Anderson won 7 percent of the popular vote, Ronald Reagan's 51 percent was translated into 91 percent of the electoral vote. In 1912— when Theodore Roosevelt mounted the most successful third-party challenge of the twentieth century—Woodrow Wilson eked out 42 percent of the popular vote but won 82 percent of the electoral vote. As a result of the typical amplified plurality, contingency elections are almost never necessary—indeed, none has been necessary since the election of 1824, which was held before the unit rule and the two-party system emerged.

Nevertheless, despite the failure of Theodore Roosevelt, George Wallace, and John Anderson, someone might mount a third-party campaign that prevents, or delays, an electoral college victory by one of the major parties. This guide sets down, as succinctly as possible, the constitutional, statutory, and parliamentary rules governing, or otherwise affecting, the choice of a president and vice president, especially in elections producing no clear majority in the electoral college. The discussion focuses on four dates significant to this choice:

• early November, when, by federal statute, electors are chosen or "appointed" (see "1. Time of appointing electors," appendix B)
• mid-December, when the electors meet in their respective states and give their votes for president and vice president (see "7. Meeting and vote of electors," appendix B)

• January 6, when the electoral votes are counted before a joint session of the House and Senate (see "15. Counting electoral votes in Congress," appendix B)

• January 20, when, under the Twentieth Amendment of the Constitution (see appendix A), the president-elect, if there is one, and the vice president-elect, if there is one, take office

Throughout this guide, we refer to January 6 as the day when Congress counts the electoral votes and to January 20 as the day when the president and vice president take office. In 1985, however, January 6 and January 20 fell on Sundays, which, since the adoption of the Twentieth Amendment in 1933, had happened only once before, in 1957. In that year the problem was resolved as follows: Senate Concurrent Resolution 1, adopted unanimously (and, apparently, without debate) on January 4, 1957, fixed 1:00 P.M. on Monday, January 7, as the time the Senate and House would meet in joint session to open and count the electoral votes. They did so meet and counted the votes and declared the winners by the usual procedures. Congress acted similarly in 1985. On November 9, 1988, even though January 6, 1989, fell on a Friday (not a Sunday), Congress, by Joint Resolution, declared that in 1989 the electoral votes would be counted on January 4, a Wednesday.

The date and time for the ending of the president's and vice president's terms are fixed in the Constitution, however, and cannot be changed by mere act of Congress. The following account of how this situation was handled in 1957 is taken from the *Congressional Quarterly Almanac, 1957:*

> President Eisenhower and Vice President Richard M. Nixon began their second terms in office after a private, three-minute swearing-in ceremony at the White House Jan. 20 and a public oath-taking at the Capitol Jan. 21. . . . Only about 80 persons, mostly relatives, close friends and high-ranking White House officials, witnessed the Jan. 20 cere-

mony. The double oath-taking was deemed necessary because the constitutional inaugural date fell on a Sunday. On orders from the President, no newsmen, radio or television stations were permitted to record the private ceremony. Only a Navy Department photographer photographed the event.[1]

We can expect future presidents and vice presidents to follow this Eisenhower-Nixon precedent.

2

How Are Electors Appointed?

November 3, 1992
November 5, 1996
November 7, 2000

Although the millions of citizens who vote in the November election rightly think that they are deciding who shall be president, only 538 persons are, under Article II and Amendment XXIII of the Constitution, entitled to vote directly for president and vice president (see appendix A). Under prevailing state laws, these 538 electors are chosen by popular vote of the people of the states and of the District of Columbia. Except in Maine and Nebraska, they are under these state laws, chosen on a general-ticket (or winner-take-all) basis. The winning electors (or slate of electors) need capture only a plurality of the popular votes within each state.[2]

How states choose their electors is, under Article II, section 1, paragraph 2 of the Constitution, determined by state legislatures (see appendix A). Congress may, by legislation, oversee the conduct of presidential elections, and the Constitution (whose rules may be enforced by the judiciary) has a good deal to say about voter eligibility in those elections. The Constitution does not, however, require electors to be chosen by popular vote of the people. The authority of the states to appoint electors was recognized by the Supreme Court in 1892.[3]

To repeat: by state law, electors in all the states are chosen by popular vote, and (except in Maine and Nebraska) these popular votes are aggregated on a statewide basis. States may divide themselves into presidential-elector districts and aggregate the votes within each district, or, like Maine and Nebraska, require some electors to be chosen in districts and some at large. In either case the electoral vote of a state can be divided and cast for more than one presidential and vice presidential candidate. The states may empower the governor to appoint electors also, or they may authorize the legislature to appoint them.

Except in an extraordinary emergency, however, a state legislature is unlikely to assume the power to appoint the electors or to grant it to the governor or any other person or group. Electors have been popularly elected since the Civil War. In fact, with one exception, South Carolina was the only state after 1824 whose legislators chose the electors; its legislature did so through 1860. The exception was Colorado; having been admitted to the Union so close to the 1876 election, it had its electors (on that occasion only) chosen by vote of the legislature.

Who Resolves Disputed Appointments?

Any disputes concerning the appointment of electors—for example, disputes about which slate of electors has received a plurality of the popular votes cast in the November election—are resolved by the states themselves. A federal statute provides that the persons designated electors by the states will be acknowledged by the Congress to be electors and eligible to vote in mid-December, for president and vice president under the following conditions:

• if a state has a law governing the "determination of any controversy or contest" concerning the election of any or all of its presidential electors

• if that law had been enacted "prior to the day fixed for the appointment of the electors" (in early November: November 3 in 1992, November 5 in 1996, November 7 in 2000)

• if the determination of that controversy or contest was made at least six days "before the time fixed for the meeting of the electors" (six days before the mid-December meeting of the electors)

This means that the popular votes cast in November are counted by state election officials and that any controversies about the casting or counting of these votes are resolved by state officials operating under state laws. (See "5. Determination of controversy as to appointment of electors," appendix B.)

The federal law authorizing the states to resolve election disputes, enacted in 1887, was intended to prevent a recurrence of the events that followed the disputed Hayes-Tilden election of 1876. When Congress met to "count" the electoral votes after that election, it was confronted with two sets of electors—one set voting for Hayes and the other for Tilden—from each of four states. The choice of a president turned on the issue of which votes were to be accepted and counted. Unable to agree, Congress, by an act approved by the president on January 29, 1877, almost three months after the election of electors, appointed a fifteen-member Electoral Commission. In due course and by a strictly partisan vote of 8–7, the commission decided in favor of the Hayes electors, thus enabling Hayes to be elected president by a margin of one electoral vote. (In Wichita Falls, Texas, between Grant and Garfield streets, and running parallel with them, there is both a Tilden Street *and* a Hayes Street, which suggests a fine sense of historical propriety, or a sharply and equally divided city council at the time this section of the city was being planned, or a doubt as to how the Electoral Commission would decide.) By enacting the law of 1887, Congress decided that in the future any such "controversy or contest" would be resolved by the states and that the determinations made by the states "shall be conclusive, and shall govern in the counting of the electoral votes as provided in the Constitution."

How the States Nominate and Bind Their Electors

As pointed out earlier, the presidential electors of each state are selected by procedures stipulated by its legislature. This section examines three aspects of these procedures: (1) how candidates for presidential electors are nominated, (2) whether the names of the individual elector candidates are printed on the ballots in November, and (3) whether the persons elected as presidential electors are bound by law to vote in the electoral college for the national nominees of their parties.

The procedures in each of the states are summarized in the table in appendix C. This table shows considerable variation among the states in their manner of nominating candidates for presidential electors. Twenty-nine states stipulate that each party's candidates for electors be chosen by state party conventions; six states and the District of Columbia require nomination by state or district party central committees; and twelve let the parties use whatever methods they wish.

In addition, there is a smattering of other methods. In California the Democrats choose their elector candidates by having each Democratic nominee for the U.S. House of Representatives designate one elector candidate and each of the two most recent Democratic nominees for the U.S. Senate designate one elector candidate. For California Republicans, the party's most recent nominees for the state constitutional offices and for the U.S. Senate, the party's leaders in each house of the state legislature, and various leaders of the state party organization select the elector candidates.

In Pennsylvania the national presidential nominee of each party names the elector candidates on his party's ticket. In Wisconsin each party's holdover members of both houses of the legislature together with its candidates for the contested legislative seats constitute the convention that chooses the elector candidates.

Forty-two states and the District of Columbia use the presidential short ballot, on which the names of the elector candidates do not appear. The ballot shows each national party's presidential and vice presidential candidates. The voter votes directly for one pair, and that vote is taken as a vote for all the elector candidates on that party's slate.

Finally, are the presidential electors bound by law to

vote in the electoral college for the presidential and vice presidential nominees who headed the slates on which the electors were elected? Twenty-six states have no such requirement. Nineteen states and the District of Columbia say that the electors are bound to vote for the national nominees heading their slate but provide no penalty for electors who do not. Only five states—New Mexico, North Carolina, Oklahoma, South Carolina, and Washington—stipulate penalties for electors who violate their pledges.

Violation of a pledge is variously described as a misdemeanor, carrying a fine of not more than $1,000 (Oklahoma), or as a fourth-degree felony (New Mexico), or as an unspecified offense carrying a fine of $1,000 (Washington). South Carolina permits any elector to take legal action to force another elector to comply with his or her pledge, but also permits a state party executive committee to release an elector from the pledge if, in its judgment, it would not be in the best interest of the state for the elector to cast the vote as pledged. North Carolina has what is probably the most effective enforcement provision: like Oklahoma, New Mexico, and Washington, it would rely on the state attorney general to initiate legal action to collect the $500 fine it would impose on the "faithless" elector, but, in addition, it provides that failure to vote as pledged shall constitute a resignation from the office of elector, that his (or her) vote not be recorded, and that another elector be appointed to cast the vote.

Three types of voting behavior are possible for electors. (1) The "faithful elector" is pledged by state law or by state party resolution to vote for his party's presidential and vice presidential candidates and casts his electoral vote accordingly. (2) The "faithless elector" is pledged in the same way but casts his electoral vote for others. (3) The "unpledged elector," who is not pledged by law or party resolution to vote for any particular candidates and is legally free to vote for anyone he chooses.

The likelihood that a significant number of electors will violate their pledges is very small. From 1789 through

1980 only fourteen unpledged electors have been chosen, and only eight electors have violated their pledges (one each in 1796, 1820, 1948, 1956, 1960, 1968, 1972, and 1976). None of the eight faithless electors was legally penalized for violating a pledge, though some suffered damage to their political reputations and careers. Because only eight of the more than 16,000 electors chosen since the first election have not honored their pledges, the faithless elector phenomenon is an occasional curiosity rather than a perennial problem.

Procedures for nominating candidates for presidential electors or for slates headed by independent or minor party presidential candidates also vary by state. Statutes pertaining to independent candidates generally require the names of the electors to be included on the nomination petition, thus giving that candidate considerable discretion in the choice of presidential elector nominees.

Whether an independent candidate is therefore in a better position than a major party candidate to dictate how his electors vote is not at all clear. In 1968 it was reported that George Wallace had obtained affidavits from all of his electors, in which they promised to vote for Wallace "or whomsoever he may direct" in the electoral college. Thus, if no candidate had received an electoral college majority, Wallace might have been able to decide the winner by giving his votes to Richard Nixon or Hubert Humphrey. Since Nixon won a majority in the electoral college, however, the Wallace pledges were never put to a test.

The Supreme Court in *Ray v. Blair* upheld the legality of pledges required by a political party from candidates for the office of presidential elector.[4] The Court did not, however, directly address the constitutional status of presidential elector pledges. It remains to be seen whether the courts will uphold the contractual relationship between presidential candidates and their electors. At present the electors retain their constitutional status of free agents, meaning that presidential candidates may advise their electors but may not compel them to vote in a specified manner.

3

For Whom Do Electors Vote?

December 14, 1992
December 16, 1996
December 18, 2000

Because most electors remain free, that is, not bound in their voting by state law, there is a good deal of room for bargaining between the November election and the meeting of the electors in mid-December—if the election does not produce a majority in the electoral college. For example, the electors for a third-party candidate who wins a plurality of the popular votes in one or more states, could cast their ballots for one of the major party candidates (or anyone else). In 1968, Hubert Humphrey could have asked his electors to vote for Richard Nixon (if Nixon had lacked an electoral college majority) rather than see Nixon bargain with George Wallace. Thus, the electoral college could well produce a winner in December that was not apparent on election day in November.

How the Ballots Are Cast

The electors appointed or chosen in November meet in their respective states in early December (December 14 in 1992, December 16 in 1996, December 18 in 2000). Each elector casts two ballots, one for president and one for vice president. Although unknown to most of the public, the names of the electors will have been certified by the governors to an official of the federal government, the archivist of the United States. A federal statute requires that this be done "as soon as practicable" after the November election. (See "6. Credentials of electors" in appendix B.) Thus, shortly after the November election, an official of the national government knows the names of the 538 persons who will meet in their respective states and in the District of Columbia in December and will vote for president and vice president. He also knows the number of popular votes cast for the successful, as well as for the unsuccessful, candidates for electors.

The persons whose names appear in the certificates sent by the governors to Washington are the electors eligible to vote for president and vice president in December. As discussed in chapter 2, any "controversy or contest" concerning the identity of these eligible electors will have been resolved by the states acting under state laws. The votes they cast, one for president and one for vice president, will be recorded in certificates, which will be sealed and sent to the president of the Senate and to the Archivist of the United States in Washington. (See "9. Certificates of votes for President and Vice President," "10. Sealing and endorsing certificates," and "11. Disposition of certificates," appendix B.)

Must the President and the Vice President Be from Different States?

At least one of the two votes cast by electors must, of course, be cast for a person who is "not an inhabitant of the same state with themselves." It is this constitutional provision that has led to the practice of political parties (and independent candidates) to nominate a candidate for president from one state and a candidate for vice president from another state.

The Constitution does not require the president and vice president to be inhabitants of different states; it merely requires electors to cast at least one ballot for someone from another state. Thus, if in 1980 the Republican party had nominated Gerald Ford to run with his fellow Californian Ronald Reagan (assuming neither changed his official residence to another state), only California electors would have been presented with a problem, and more precisely, only California Republican electors. They would have had to vote for Reagan and, say, Jack Kemp, or, say, Jack Kemp and Gerald Ford; they would not have been permitted to vote for a ticket comprising *both* Reagan and Ford.

In 1990, this issue arose with the speculation that Secretary of State James Baker might run with his fellow Texan George Bush. Of course, in this era of residential mobility and multiple residences, this problem is unlikely to arise; it is a simple matter to change one's legal residence.

4

How Are the Electoral Votes Counted?

January 6

The certificates containing the votes cast in their respective states by the 538 electors in December will be opened by the president of the Senate on January 6, before a joint session of the new House and the new Senate, the members of which (under the Twentieth Amendment) will themselves have been sworn in on January 3. (See appendix A.) The certificates are identified and counted by tellers appointed by the House and the Senate, and announced by states in alphabetical order.

According to the Twelfth Amendment of the Constitution (see appendix A), the person having the greatest number of votes for president, if such number is a majority of the electors appointed, shall be president; and the person having the greatest number of votes for vice president, if such number is a majority of the electors appointed, shall be vice president. Assuming each state "appoints" the number of electors to which it is entitled, the total of electors will be 538 and the majority required for election will be 270.

Who Counts What?

The tellers read "certificates and papers purporting to be certificates of the electoral votes." The president of the Senate calls for objections, if any, to these certificates or papers as they are read.[5] The statute provides that objections must be made in writing, must state "clearly and concisely, and without argument, the ground thereof," and must be signed by at least one member of the House and one member of the Senate.

When objections are filed, both houses retire to separate sessions to decide whether the questioned certificates are to be counted or rejected. Under the statute, both houses have to reject a challenged electoral ballot for the objection to prevail. The statute says that Congress shall not reject any "electoral vote or votes from any state which shall have been regularly given by electors whose appointment has been lawfully certified," but it does not define "regularly given." (See "15. Counting electoral votes in Congress," appendix B.)

These procedures were used for the first time on January 6, 1969. Representative James O'Hara (Democrat, Michigan), Senator Edmund Muskie (Democrat, Maine), thirty-seven other representatives, and six other senators objected in writing to the vote cast by Dr. Lloyd Bailey, a North Carolina elector who had been on the Republican slate but who voted for George Wallace and Curtis LeMay rather than for Richard Nixon and Spiro Agnew. By roll call votes, both houses rejected the challenge and upheld the vote cast by Bailey.

It might be concluded from this example that a "regularly given vote"—which is a vote the Congress must count—means no more than a vote cast by an elector whose name had been certified by the governor of the state to the archivist of the United States. Under this interpretation a list of certified electors from each state will on January 6 be in the hands of the Congress, whose only function would be to see that the votes were cast by the electors whose names appear on those lists.

The term "regularly given" could, however, be interpreted more expansively by a future Congress, especially a Congress confronted with faithless electors whose votes, unlike Bailey's, would determine the outcome of an election. The term does, after all, appear in the 1887 statute written by Congress. But if Congress were to refuse to count a vote cast by a faithless elector—for example, a vote cast for a third-party candidate by an elector pledged to vote for a Republican or Democratic candidate—it would be interpreting more than statutory language: it would be making a constitutional judgment.

Prior to the 1887 law, some authorities (including Abraham Lincoln) understood that the power to resolve disputes concerning what electoral votes to count belonged exclusively to Congress. In his Message to Congress of February 8, 1865, President Lincoln wrote as follows:

> The joint resolution, entitled "Joint Resolution declaring certain States not entitled to representation in the electoral college," has been signed by the executive, in deference to the view implied in its passage and presentation to him. In his own view, however, the two Houses of Congress, convened under the twelfth article of the Constitution, have complete power to exclude from counting all electoral votes deemed by them to be illegal; and it is not competent for the executive to defeat or obstruct that power by a veto, as would be the case if his action were at all essential in the matter. He disclaims all right of the executive to interfere in any way in the matter of canvassing or counting electoral votes. . . .[6]

If the results of the November election are disputed and Congress receives more than one list of electors, and if that dispute had not been resolved according to the laws of the state, then the two houses, acting concurrently, will decide who are the eligible electors. (See "5. Determination of controversy as to appointment of electors," appendix B.) If they disagree, the votes cast by the persons whose names appear on the list signed by the governor of the state will be counted.

19

5

What If No One Has a Majority?

January 20

Once the Congress has met and counted and certified the electoral votes, the Twelfth Amendment of the Constitution sets the basic provisions for decision if no presidential candidate has received the requisite majority:

> From the persons having the highest numbers not exceeding three on the list of those voted for as President, the House of Representatives shall choose immediately, by ballot, the President. But in choosing the President, the votes shall be taken by states, the representation from each state having one vote; a quorum for this purpose shall consist of a member or members from two-thirds of the states, and a majority of all the states shall be necessary to a choice.

The House Chooses a President

Should a presidential election be thrown into Congress for decision, there are precedents, rules, laws, and procedures for making decisions—but also much room for the particular Congress to determine its own format and rules.

Provisions in the Twelfth and Twentieth Amendments of the Constitution determine the basic role of the House of Representatives in this process. With regard to the mechanics of the House decision, the House, as in other matters, sets its own rules and procedures. The precedents set by the House in February 1825 in deciding the election of 1824 provide some guidance. (See appendix D.)

The House could follow these precedents, or if it wished, ignore them and draw up a new set of procedures.

The new procedures would be unlikely to differ greatly from the 1825 set, except in one key respect—in 1825, the old, or lame-duck, House made the presidential selection. The Twentieth Amendment changed the date of convention of the new Congress from March 20 to January 3, thus seating the new Congress before the January 6 statutory date for counting the electoral votes in Congress. Congress could conceivably set this statutory date back, empowering the old Congress to make the presidential decision. That is most unlikely, however, particularly since the record of deliberation on the Twentieth Amendment reflects a clear intention to have this decision in the hands of the new Congress.

Of the specific precedents from 1825, one is of particular significance: the requirement of a majority of a state's whole delegation to vote for a candidate in order for the state vote to be cast. If no candidate got a majority, the state was recorded as divided, and no vote was cast. In the 102nd Congress, taking office in January 1991, thirty-one state delegations had Democratic majorities, ten had Republican majorities, eight were evenly divided between the two parties, and one, Vermont, had an independent as its sole member. If a few House seats shifted from one party to the other in, for example, the 1992 elections, or if only a few votes by House members were cast for a third-party candidate in state delegations, enough divided states could be created to prevent any presidential candidate from getting the twenty-six state votes needed to win.

The Senate Chooses a Vice President

The Twelfth Amendment of the Constitution also sets the basic provisions for decision if no vice presidential candidate has received the requisite majority of electoral votes: "from the two highest numbers on the list, the Senate shall choose the Vice President; a quorum for the purpose shall

21

consist of two-thirds of the whole number of Senators, and a majority of the whole number shall be necessary to a choice." The Senate has selected a vice president once, in 1837, when President-elect Martin Van Buren's running mate, Richard Johnson, because of a personal scandal, received one fewer than a majority of electoral votes. He was, however, elected by the Senate.

Unlike members of the House, senators vote as individuals, not as part of a state delegation, and they choose between the top two candidates, not the top three. Moreover, the requirements for a quorum in the Senate—two-thirds of the full Senate, or, at present, sixty-seven senators—are more stringent than in the House, where only one member from two-thirds of the states is needed. Thus, a boycott by members of one party in the Senate could prevent a choice of vice president, if that party had more than the thirty-four senators needed to block a quorum.

6

What If No One Has Been Chosen by Inauguration Day?

The Twentieth Amendment of the Constitution fixes the end of the terms of the president and vice president at noon on January 20. If a president has been chosen by that time, he will be sworn in. If a president has not been chosen, but there is a vice president-elect, the vice president becomes acting president until the House selects the president in the manner described earlier.

The Presidential Succession Act

The Presidential Succession Act of 1948 comes into play under any of the following conditions:

- if the House fails to choose a president and the Senate fails to choose a vice president
- if the president-elect and vice president-elect both die
- if both are discovered after January 6 to be constitutionally unqualified to hold office[7]

(See "19. Vacancy in offices of both President and Vice President; officers eligible to act," appendix B.)

The next in line after the vice president to serve as acting president is the speaker of the House, who in turn is followed by the president pro tempore of the Senate. They may act as president, however, only if they meet the legal requirements for the presidency, spelled out in Article II of the Constitution. In addition, Article I of the Constitution bars members of the House and Senate from holding any other federal office. The Presidential Succession Act specifically interprets this to mean that the speaker or president pro tempore must resign from the House or Senate to serve as acting president.

Since the Presidential Succession Act requires the acting president to relinquish that position as soon as a president or vice president is chosen, the speaker and president pro tempore might well choose not to resign from Congress to become acting president. If that happens, the process then moves on to qualified cabinet officers in the following order: secretaries of state, treasury, and defense, attorney general, secretaries of interior, agriculture, commerce, labor, health and human services, housing and urban development, transportation, energy, education, and veterans' affairs. Since cabinet officers stay in office until they resign or are discharged by the president or acting president, the person who would become acting president under this set of contingencies would be a cabinet officer from the previous administration.

Only officers confirmed by the Senate (not, for example, an acting secretary) and not under impeachment by the House may become acting president. Confirmed cabinet officers will be passed over if they fail to qualify as president, and subsequent qualification of the officer thus passed over (such as by turning thirty-five or by reaching his fourteenth year of residency in this country) would not result in a change of acting president. A later decision by a qualified speaker or president pro tempore to resign from Congress would, however, displace the former cabinet officer and make the speaker or president pro tempore the acting president until a vice president or president is named or until the presidential term expires, whichever comes first.

7

What If a Major Party Candidate Dies or Resigns?

If a candidate nominated by a political party dies or resigns before the date fixed for the choice of presidential electors (that is, in November), the national committee of the affected party will meet and choose a new presidential or vice presidential candidate. Article III of the Charter and Bylaws of the Democratic Party and rule 27 of the rules of the Republican Party permit the national committees so to act. (See appendix E.)

In 1912, both President William H. Taft and Vice President James S. Sherman were renominated at the June Republican convention. Vice President Sherman died October 30, and the Republican National Committee chose another candidate, but not until after the November election. The committee substituted Nicholas Murray Butler, and the eight Republican electors cast their ballots for him in the December voting.

In 1972, Senator Thomas Eagleton was nominated July 13 as the candidate for vice president at the Democratic national convention. Stories began circulating almost immediately about Senator Eagleton's problems of mental strain some years before and his three hospitalizations. At first, presidential nominee George McGovern supported Eagleton's continuation on the ticket, but Senator Eagleton finally withdrew at the end of July. On August 8 the Democratic National Committee substituted R. Sargent Shriver as the new nominee for vice president.

Death or Resignation after the Election

If the death or resignation occurred between the November election and mid-December, the day the electors cast their ballots, the national committee of the party affected would probably proceed as it would if the candidate died or resigned before the November election—assuming there was time to convene the committee. In any event, no legal problem would arise because (leaving aside the question of electors bound by state law to cast a ballot for a named candidate) the electors, under the Constitution, are free to vote for whomever they choose.

If the death or resignation occurred between January 6 and January 20, the case would be governed by the Twentieth Amendment of the Constitution. Section 3 of the Amendment reads:

> If, at the time fixed for the beginning of the term of the President, the President elect shall have died, the Vice President elect shall become President. . . . and the Congress may by law provide for the case wherein neither a President elect nor a Vice President elect shall have qualified, declaring who shall then act as President, or the manner in which one who is to act shall be selected. . . .

Thus, if both the president-elect and the vice president-elect were to die during this period, the law enacted by Congress under the authority of this amendment (the Presidential Succession Act) would take effect. (See "19. Vacancy in offices of both President and Vice President; officers eligible to act," appendix B.)

There is some question concerning the consequences if the death occurs between mid-December and January 6. Would there be a president-elect and a vice president-elect during this period? If so, the Twentieth Amendment governs the case, and, if the president-elect dies, the person receiving the majority of electoral votes cast for vice president—or, if no one receives a majority, the person chosen by the Senate on January 6 to be vice president—becomes president. In either case, that person will be vice president-elect, and, as the Twentieth Amendment says, if, at the time fixed for the beginning of the terms of the president, the president-elect shall have died, "the Vice President-elect shall become President."

There will probably be no president-elect, however, until the electoral votes are counted and announced by Congress on January 6. Although the electors will have voted and the country will know—or will think it knows—whether anyone has received a majority, those votes will be under seal and will not be known officially until they are opened by the Congress. The president of the Senate will "thereupon announce the state of the vote, which announcement shall be deemed a sufficient declaration of the persons, if any, elected President and Vice President of the United States. . . ." (See "15. Counting electoral votes in Congress," appendix B.)

Moreover, the same statute also requires the president of the Senate, when opening "the certificates and papers purporting to be certificates of the electoral votes" of each state in turn, to "call for objections, if any." The statute then specifies the manner of dealing with those objections. Only after they have been dealt with, or only after all the questions concerning the validity of the certificates have been resolved, may the president of the Senate "announce the state of the vote." It follows, therefore, that only then will there be a president-elect and a vice president-elect. The Twentieth Amendment cannot govern the case of a candidate's death occurring between mid-December and January 6; it can only be governed by the Twelfth Amendment.

The death or resignation of a candidate during this period would be of political concern only if the candidate had been the choice of a majority of electors, or if no candidate had won a majority. In either case the choice of a president would devolve upon the House (or, in the choice of a vice

27

president, upon the Senate). This conclusion rests on the following clause of the Twelfth Amendment: "and if no person [living] have such majority, then from the persons having the highest numbers not exceeding three on the list of those voted for as President, the House of Representatives shall choose immediately, by ballot, the President." Thus, to be concrete, if the Republican, Democratic, and some third-party candidate all win electoral votes, and if the one winning a majority were to die or resign between mid-December and January 6, the House would, on January 6, choose a president from the other two.

What Is *Not* Covered

Section 4 of the Twentieth Amendment provides that

> Congress may by law provide for the case of the death of any of the persons from whom the House of Representatives may choose a President whenever the right of choice shall have devolved upon them, and for the case of the death of any of the persons from whom the Senate may choose a Vice President whenever the right of choice shall have devolved upon them.

Unfortunately, Congress has not enacted such a law. The Presidential Succession Act, authorized by section 3 of the Twentieth Amendment, meets the cases of the death of a president or president-elect and of a vice president or vice president-elect, but not the cases of the death "of any of the persons" from whom the House and Senate may choose a president or vice president. In enacting the Presidential Succession Act, Congress may have thought it was providing for the case of a death of any of the persons from whom the House may choose a president and the Senate a vice president. If the reading here given to the terms "president-elect" and "vice president-elect" is correct, however, that act does not cover the case.

Congress could, of course, choose to ignore the

winning candidate's death and proceed to name him president-elect. Then, the president-elect having died, the vice president-elect would, under the Twentieth Amendment, become president. Congress might reason that this outcome is in accordance with the popular will or, at least, does not thwart it.

8

Conclusion

In a democracy, the people, and more precisely, a majority of the people, are expected to choose the persons holding the highest political offices. Although not by constitutional design, this is what in fact happens in the United States. Only when the electoral college fails to produce a majority does the choice of a president devolve upon some other body. That has not happened since 1825, and only once in our modern history (1888) has the candidate winning the majority of the popular vote failed to win a majority of the electoral vote.

As the proponents of direct election are quite right to remind us, there is no guarantee that the system will continue to produce results in accord with the will of a simple majority of the voters. Nevertheless, on the basis of the record, the friends of majority-rule democracy have no reason to complain of the method by which this country chooses its presidents (see chapter 9).

A country governed by law can also be expected to have provided legally binding rules governing unusual cases of succession to the highest offices, and this, too, the United States has done. That much should be made clear by this guide. The various constitutional, statutory, and parliamentary rules elucidated and in some instances interpreted in this study govern almost every conceivable contingency. So long as these rules are followed, this country will not suffer a crisis of succession.

Stated differently, adherence to these legally prescribed provisions will produce a president and a vice president with unchallengeable constitutional and legal claims to those offices. The importance of this cannot be exaggerated in a world where the law of succession is often bent to the dictates of force. The friends of constitutional government have no reason to complain of the method by which this country chooses its presidents.

PART TWO

How the Electoral College Has Evolved

Essays by
Norman J. Ornstein
and
Martin Diamond

9

Three Disputed Elections

Norman J. Ornstein

Three presidential elections in American history have raised both controversy and constitutional question marks—the elections of 1800, 1824, and 1876. The controversy in 1800 resulted in a constitutional amendment, and the one in 1876 in major legislation to change the process of presidential succession.

The Election of 1800

The original Constitution did not provide for separate ballots for president and vice president. Electors voted for two candidates, and the candidate who received the most electoral votes (if a majority) became president, while the candidate finishing second became vice president. If two candidates tied with a majority of electoral votes, then the House of Representatives would vote to break the tie.

In 1800, the Federalist party's congressional caucus nominated John Adams as its presidential candidate for a second term and South Carolina's Charles Cotesworth Pinckney as his running mate. Pinckney had also been paired with Adams in 1796 but fell short of second place in the electoral vote. The Democratic-Republican Thomas Jefferson was therefore elected vice president.

Portions of this account of the election of 1824 are adapted from an article in *Fortune* magazine in 1980 by Norman Ornstein and Richard Brody.

The congressional caucus of the Democratic-Republican party nominated Vice President Thomas Jefferson for president, pairing him with Aaron Burr. After the electors assembled in their respective states on December 4, it became clear that the Democrat-Republicans had prevailed, but Jefferson and Burr received an equal number of electoral votes, 73. Adams received 65, and Pinckney 64.

The presidency therefore had to be decided by a lame-duck House of Representatives, which still had a Federalist majority. Rather than following the Democratic-Republication party's choice for president, the Federalists complicated the selection with mischief-making and political maneuvering.

Because Thomas Jefferson was the most visible and capable foe of the Federalists, there was substantial sentiment in the party to pass him by and give the presidency to Burr, a man they saw as less formidable and more pliable. At the same time the party would be sowing deep dissension within the opposition. But the patriotism and honor of Federalist Alexander Hamilton ultimately prevented that strategy from succeeding. Hamilton's personal relationship with Burr, at that time, was quite cordial, while his relationship with Jefferson was bitter. Hamilton wrote, "If there be a man in the world I ought to hate, it is Jefferson. With Burr I have always been personally well. But the public good must be paramount to every private consideration."

Congress assembled on February 11, 1801, for the electoral count. As the vice president and the presiding officer of the Senate, Jefferson received the votes from the tellers and announced them. The electoral votes of Georgia were not authenticated by the signatures of any electors, either outside or inside the envelope, which merely contained a statement that four votes had been cast for Jefferson and Burr. Uncertain how to handle this, the tellers handed the envelope to Jefferson, who declared that Georgia had cast four votes for him and four votes for Burr, avoiding any interpretation that might have favored him or cast additional doubt on the vote.

The formal count in the House thus replicated the earlier reports, and the House itself began to vote. There were 58 Federalists and 48 Democratic-Republicans in the 106-member House of Representatives at the time; had the vote been by member, there is little doubt that Burr would have won. But the Constitution provided that the votes would be cast by states. On the first ballot, Jefferson won eight states, Burr, six, and two, Maryland and Vermont, were equally divided. From February 11 to February 17, thirty-five votes were taken with the same result. The opportunities for vote trading and influence peddling were enormous, but neither candidate succumbed or succeeded. Hamilton's influence finally broke the logjam. On the thirty-sixth ballot, many Federalists declined to vote; the two deadlocked states went for Jefferson, while Delaware and South Carolina, previously for Burr, now deadlocked themselves. The final count was ten states for Jefferson and four states, all in New England, for Burr. Burr automatically became vice president.

A few years later, after Hamilton had intervened in New York politics to stop Burr once again, their personal relationship deteriorated until they met in a duel—perhaps the most infamous in American history—which resulted in the tragic death of Founding Father Alexander Hamilton.

The dangers inherent in the original system of double-balloting became clear with the Jefferson-Burr controversy. Momentum for an amendment to allow separate electoral votes for president and vice president began to build immediately after the vote in the House. The Twelfth Amendment to the Constitution was approved by Congress in December 1803 and ratified by the states in time for the next presidential election.

The Election of 1824

Five serious contenders emerged for the presidency as 1824 approached: John C. Calhoun and William H. Crawford from the South; John Quincy Adams from the Northeast; and Henry Clay and Andrew Jackson from the West.[1] Calhoun dropped out of consideration in 1824 to run for vice president, leaving four. William H. Crawford of Georgia was Treasury secretary under President Monroe. He received the Republican congressional caucus nomination, but with only sixty-six of the Republican members of Congress in attendance, barely a third of the total, the nomination was widely attacked as illegitimate and unconstitutional; at the same time, a number of newspapers attacked the power of "King Caucus" in general. The other presidential candidates received their nominations through other venues: Adams was nominated by the legislatures of several states in New England; Clay was picked by the legislature of Kentucky; Jackson was nominated by the Tennessee legislature and by nominating conventions held across the country.

In a campaign characterized more by questions of personality than issues, and dominated by personal attacks on the candidates by partisan newspapers, no single strong candidate for president emerged. Twenty-four states cast electoral votes; 131 votes were necessary for a majority. Andrew Jackson led with 99, polling 152,901 popular votes (44.3 percent of those cast); he carried Pennsylvania, New Jersey, most of the South, and the new West, except for Ohio. Adams received 84 electoral votes and 114,023 (30 percent) popular votes, carrying New York and New England. Crawford received 41 electoral votes, carrying Georgia, Virginia, and eight scattered others.

Clay, to his bitter disappointment, finished fourth, four behind Crawford despite winning more popular votes than the Treasury secretary (13.2 percent to 12.5 percent). Clay won all the electoral votes of Ohio, Missouri, and his native Kentucky and four from New York. Had Clay, the veteran speaker of the House, received only three electoral votes from the hodgepodge of electors who went for the ill and paralytic Crawford—and questions were raised about the legitimacy of several of those votes—he would without doubt have been elected president by the House of

Representatives. But the Constitution limited the choice to the top three candidates, rendering him ineligible.

In January 1825 the contest shifted to the House, which proceeded to ballot by state. No rules existed for the vote, so the House directed each state vote to be cast according to the preference of an absolute majority of the state's congressmen.

Though the speaker, Henry Clay, had been deprived through political machinations of a chance at the prize, his role was far from over. Clay was not a strong admirer of any of the three choices, but he eagerly assumed the role of kingmaker. Crawford's health condition removed him from serious consideration, even though his issue positions were closest to Clay's. Clay had opposed Adams regularly during Adam's tenure as Monroe's secretary of state, although they agreed on the Monroe Doctrine. Jackson assiduously courted Clay, but, to Clay, he was not a trained statesman, sophisticated in the ways of statecraft, while Adams, despite their differences, was.

Clay met with Adams on Sunday evening, January 9, and soon rumors were circulating that Clay had been promised the State Department if he delivered the votes of Ohio and Kentucky—states Clay had won in the election. Clay denied the charges, calling his accuser "a base and infamous calumniator, a dastard, and a liar." Nevertheless, on January 24, Clay and a majority of the Ohio and Kentucky delegates announced their support for Adams.

Several states, though committed to Adams on the first ballot, meant to defect to Jackson on a later round of voting. To win, Adams needed a first ballot victory, and New York's vote would ensure it. But the New York delegation was split. The deciding ballot was in the hands of kindly old Stephen Van Rensselaer, who had pledged support to all three candidates. In the end, with some help from Daniel Webster, Adams managed to win Van Rensselaer's vote—and with it the White House.

Later Van Rensselaer claimed that it was divine intervention, not pressure, that prompted his vote for Adams.

As New York began to vote, he claimed, he had bent his head in prayer and spied on the floor a ballot for Adams. He took this as a sign from heaven, and voted accordingly.

Soon thereafter, Henry Clay was named secretary of state. Although much evidence would suggest that Clay's support for Adams had other, legitimate roots, it did not stop an uproar of protest. Senator John Randolph of Virginia was so outraged that he hurled public insults at Clay, calling him a "blackleg," the term for a dishonest gambler. In response to this public humiliation, Clay met Randolph in a duel on the banks of the Potomac, armed with pistols, each accompanied by seconds and by a surgeon. Shots were fired, but the only casualty was the skirt of Randolph's coat. The duelers then chose to settle their differences with a handshake, and within a week they had exchanged cards and resumed social relations.

Jackson did not resume any relationship with Clay. He bitterly wrote friends, "Was there ever such a barefaced corruption in any country before?" Four years later, Jackson, running a populist campaign against the sort of backroom politics that had elected Adams, won the presidential election of 1828 by a landslide.

The Election of 1876

The election of 1876, ironically America's centennial year, was perhaps the most controversial in American history. It was not decided in the House of Representatives, but rather by a special Electoral Commission formed to settle the controversy over disputed electoral votes.

At their conventions, the Republicans and the Democrats both picked as their candidates well-respected, reform governors. The Republicans, meeting in Cincinnati, chose Ohio Governor Rutherford B. Hayes, known for his opposition to the spoils system. The Democrats, meeting in St. Louis, picked New York Governor Samuel J. Tilden, who had broken both Tammany Hall and the infamous Canal Ring.

There were few major differences in the positions of the two candidates on the top issues of the time. The campaign, focusing on personalities, became bitter and dirty. Each side hurled insults and lies at the other. Hayes was accused of stealing the pay of dead soldiers in the Civil War and shooting his mother in a fit of insanity, while Tilden, among other things, was called a drunkard, thief, syphilitic, liar, and swindler.

In the aftermath of the election, it appeared that Tilden had won. He had received 264,000 more popular votes than Hayes and outdistanced him in electoral votes by 184 to 165. With twenty electoral votes still outstanding, and 185 required to win, Tilden needed only one more to clinch a victory. Even Hayes thought he had lost the election when he retired on election night.

But the leadership of the Republican party was unwilling to give up. Party Chairman Zachariah Chandler and his associates began to exert pressure on the remaining states, South Carolina, Florida, and Louisiana, and on one of Oregon's three votes. Chandler publicly claimed all three of Oregon's electoral votes, and sent telegrams to Republican officials in the other three states, all at the time under carpetbag rule, asking them to hold their states and saying, "Hayes is elected if we have carried South Carolina, Florida, and Louisiana."

Chandler then claimed that Hayes had 185 electoral votes and was elected president. Near chaos ensued. President Grant had to send troops to keep the peace in areas where the votes were being tabulated. There was bribery, forgery, and ballot-box stuffing on both sides. In the end, multiple sets of returns were sent to Washington from the three Southern states involved. The struggle over the disputed votes lasted from election day, November 8, 1876, until March 2, 1877.

The Constitution does not outline specific procedures to be followed in the case of conflicting returns from any state. The Democratic House of Representatives would not agree to let the Republican Senate's president arbitrate, nor would the Republican Senate leave the decision to the Democratic House. Congress compromised by creating a fifteen-member bipartisan Electoral Commission, consisting of five senators, five representatives, and five Supreme Court justices, to decide which candidate had won the disputed votes. Seven were to be Democrats, and seven Republicans, while the fifteenth vote would be cast by Justice David Davis, universally regarded as an independent. At the last minute, however, he was elected to the Senate by the Illinois legislature, and became ineligible. The Republican Justice Joseph Bradley replaced him. Although the Democrats believed he would be nonpartisan, he voted with his Republican colleagues on every significant question. Thus, the commission split eight to seven consistently in favor of Hayes.

The electoral count began in Congress on February 1 (changed from the second Wednesday in February for this one election) and the proceedings continued until March 2. States were called in alphabetical order. When a disputed state was called, objections were raised to both Tilden and Hayes electors. The question was then referred to the electoral commission; in every instance it voted eight to seven for Hayes. The Democratic House rejected the commission's decision, but the Republican Senate upheld it, and under the rules, the decision stood.

The country ultimately acquiesced in the decision, as did Tilden, who nonetheless believed until his death that he had been duly elected president. Serious violence, however, nearly marred this election. Justice Bradley's life was threatened, and his house had to be placed under guard. Hayes, too, was threatened and even fired upon one night while eating dinner with his family. The bullet missed Hayes and lodged in the library wall. Northern Democrats were enraged by the actions of the electoral commission, and the House of Representatives launched an investigation, which found flagrant fraud by Republicans in the South—but also uncovered instances of Democratic bribery and vote abuse.

The real end to the crisis came with the Compromise

of 1877, in which Southern Democrats accepted the electoral commission's result and Hayes promised to end Reconstruction by removing Republican carpetbag governments from Southern states. Southern Democratic promises to protect the interests of Negroes in their states were soon ignored, and the post-Civil War era, and along with it civil rights, came to an end.

A decade later, in 1887, Congress finally settled on a procedure to be followed for disputed electoral votes. (See appendix B.) The Electoral Count Act placed the final authority in the states themselves for determining the validity and legality of their choice of electors. A concurrent majority in both houses of Congress would be required to reject any electoral votes.

10

The Electoral College and the American Idea of Democracy

Martin Diamond

In 1967, a distinguished commission of the American Bar Association recommended that the Electoral College be scrapped and replaced by a nationwide popular vote for the president, with provision for a runoff election between the top two candidates in the event no candidate received at least 40 percent of the popular vote. This recommendation was passed by the House in 1969, came close to passage in the Senate in 1970, and is now once again upon us. It is this proposal that has just been endorsed by President Carter and that is being pressed upon Congress under the leadership of Senator Bayh.

The theme of this attack upon the Electoral College is well summarized in a much-quoted sentence from the 1967 ABA Report: "The electoral college method of electing a President of the United States is archaic, undemocratic, complex, ambiguous, indirect, and dangerous."[1] These six charges may seem a bit harsh on a system that has worked well for a very long time, but they do provide a convenient topical outline for a brief defense of the basic principles and procedures of the Electoral College.

This essay was originally published as a booklet by the American Enterprise Institute in 1977.

An "Archaic" System?

The word "archaic" evokes all those Herblock and other cartoons that portray the Electoral College (or any other feature of the Constitution that is being caricatured) as a deaf, decrepit old fogey left over from the colonial era. This is the characteristic rhetoric and imagery of contemporary criticism of our now nearly two-centuries-old Constitution. But we ought not (and perhaps lawyers, especially, ought not) acquiesce too readily in the prejudice that whatever is old is archaic, in the ABA's pejorative use of that word. On the contrary, it may be argued that the proper political prejudice, if we are to have one, ought to be in favor of the long-persisting, of the tried and true— that our first inclination in constitutional matters ought to be that old is good and older is better. We should remind ourselves of some Aristotelian wisdom reformulated by James Madison in *Federalist* No. 49, when he warned that tinkering with the Constitution would deprive the system of government of "that veneration which time bestows on everything, and without which perhaps the wisest and freest governments would not possess the requisite stability."

In other words, a long-standing constitutional arrangement secures, by its very age, that habitual popular acceptance which is an indispensable ingredient in constitutional legitimacy, that is, in the power of a constitution to be accepted and lived under by free men and women. By this reasoning, we should preserve the Electoral College—barring truly serious harm actually experienced under it—simply on grounds of its nearly two-centuries-long history of tranquil popular acceptance. We who have seen so many free constitutions fail because they proved to be mere parchment, unrooted in the hearts and habits of the people, should be responsive to Madison's understated warning; we should readily agree that it would not be a "superfluous advantage" even to the most perfectly devised constitution to have the people's habitual acceptance on its side.[2]

But it is not necessary, in defense of the Electoral College, to rely on such sober (but startling nowadays) reasoning as that of Madison, because the Electoral College happens not to be an archaic element of our constitutional system. Not only is it not at all archaic, but one might say that it is the very model of up-to-date constitutional flexibility. Perhaps no other feature of the Constitution has had a greater capacity for dynamic historical adaptiveness. The electors became nullities; presidential elections became dramatic national contests; the federal elements in the process became strengthened by the general-ticket practice (that is, winner-take-all); modern mass political parties developed; campaigning moved from rather rigid sectionalism to the complexities of a modern technological society—and all this occurred tranquilly and legitimately within the original constitutional framework, as modified by the Twelfth Amendment. The Electoral College thus has experienced an immense historical evolution. But the remarkable fact is that while it now operates in historically transformed ways, in ways not at all as the framers intended, it nonetheless still operates largely to the ends that they intended. What more could one ask of a constitutional provision?

To appreciate why the original electoral provisions proved so adaptable, we have to recollect what the original intention was. To do that, we have first to get something out of our heads, namely, the widespread notion that the intention behind the Electoral College was undemocratic, that the main aim was to remove the election from the people and place it in the hands of wise, autonomous, detached electors who, without reference to the popular will, would choose the man they deemed best for the job. Indeed, that is what the "archaic" charge really comes down to.

What is truly odd about this view is that the Electoral College *never* functioned in the archaically undemocratic manner we assume had been intended. In the first two elections, every single elector followed the known popular preference and cast a ballot for Washington. In 1796, every single elector cast a basically mandated ballot for either Adams or Jefferson, the two recognized choices of the electorate. And from that time on, electors have functioned for all practical purposes as the mandated agents of popular choice. Now if the framers were as smart as they are made out to be, how did it happen that their archaically "elitist" instrumentality was so soon, so wholly, perverted? The answer is simple: It was not. The Electoral College never was fundamentally intended to operate in an undemocratic way. Rather, it was from the start thoroughly compatible with the democratic development that immediately ensued.

The device of independent electors as a substitute for direct popular election was hit upon for three reasons, none of which supports the thesis that the intention was fundamentally undemocratic. First and above all, the electors were not devised as an undemocratic substitute for the popular will, but rather as a nationalizing substitute for the state legislatures. In short, the Electoral College, like so much else in the Constitution, was the product of the give-and-take and the compromises between the large and the small states, or more precisely, between the confederalists—those who sought to retain much of the Articles of Confederation—and those who advocated a large, primarily national republic. It will be remembered that there was a great struggle at the Constitutional Convention over this issue, which was the matrix out of which many of the main constitutional provisions emerged. As they did regarding the House of Representatives and the Senate, the confederalists fought hard to have the president selected by the state legislatures or by some means that retained the primacy of the states as states. It was to fend off this confederalizing threat that the leading framers, Madison, James Wilson, and Gouverneur Morris, hit upon the Electoral College device. As a matter of fact, their own first choice was for a straight national popular vote; Wilson introduced that idea, and Madison and Morris endorsed it.[3] But when the "states righters" vehemently rejected it, Wilson, Madison, and Morris settled on the device of popularly elected electors. The Electoral College, thus, in its genesis and inspiration, was not an antidemocratic but an anti-states-rights device, a way of keeping the election from the state politicians and giving it to the people.[4]

Second, the system of electors also had to be devised because most of the delegates to the Convention feared not democracy itself, but only that a straightforward national election was "impracticable" in a country as large as the United States, given the poor internal communications it then had.[5] Many reasonably feared that, in these circumstances, the people simply could not have the national information about available candidates to make any real choice, let alone an intelligent one. And small-state partisans feared that, given this lack of information, ordinary voters would vote for favorite sons, with the result that large-state candidates would always win the presidential pluralities.[6] How seriously concerned the framers were with this "communications gap" is shown by the famous faulty mechanism in the original provisions (the one that made possible the Jefferson-Burr deadlock in 1801). Each elector was originally to cast two votes, but without specifying which was for president and which for vice president. The Constitution required that at least one of these two votes be for a non-home-state candidate, the intention being to force the people and their electors to cast at least one electoral vote for a truly "continental" figure. Clearly, then, what the framers were seeking was not an undemocratic way to substitute elite electors for the popular will; rather, as they claimed, they were trying to find a practicable way to extract from the popular will a nonparochial choice for the president.

The third reason for the electoral scheme likewise had nothing to do with frustrating democracy, but rather with the wide variety of suffrage practices in the states. Madison dealt with this problem at the Constitutional Convention on July 19, 1787. While election by "the people was in his opinion the fittest in itself," there was a serious circumstantial difficulty. "The right of suffrage was much more diffusive in the Northern than the Southern states; and the latter could have no influence in the election on the score of the Negroes. The substitution of electors obviated this difficulty."[7] That is, the electoral system would take care of the discrepancies between state voting population and total population of the states until, as Madison hoped and expected, slavery would be eliminated and suffrage discrepancies gradually disappeared. Again the intention was to find the most practical means in the circumstances to secure a popular choice of the president.

These were the main reasons, then, why the leading framers settled for the electoral system instead of a national popular election, and none may fairly be characterized as undemocratic. But it must be admitted that the electoral device would not occur to us nowadays as a way to solve these practical problems that the founding generation faced, because we insist on more unqualifiedly populistic political instruments than they did. All of the founding generation were far more prepared than we to accept devices and processes that, to use their terms, refined or filtered the popular will; and a few of the founders—Hamilton, for example—did vainly hope that the electors would exercise such a degree of autonomy in choosing the president as would perhaps exceed any reasonable democratic standard. This is what makes it easy for us to believe that the Electoral College was conceived undemocratically, rather than as a legitimately democratic response in the circumstances. But any fair and full reading of the evidence demands the conclusion suggested here: the majority of the Convention, and especially the leading architects of the Constitution, conceived the Electoral College simply as the most practical means by which to secure a free, democratic choice of an independent and effective chief executive.

Thus, the essential spirit of the Electoral College, like that of the Constitution in general, was fundamentally

49

democratic from the outset. That is why its mechanisms were so readily adaptable to the immense democratic developments of the last two centuries, the while preserving on balance certain unique principles of the American idea of democracy. And that is why, in defending the Electoral College, we are not clinging to an archaic eighteenth century institution. Rather, we are defending an electoral system that, because of its dynamic adaptiveness to changing circumstances, remains the most valuable way for us to choose a president.

The ABA's "archaic" charge is in fact an indictment of the electors as undemocratic. In dealing with that indictment, then, we seem to have anticipated the ABA's express charge that the Electoral College is "undemocratic." The chief contemporary attack on the Electoral College, however, has little to do with the autonomous elector or, as is said, the "faithless elector." The autonomous elector could be amended out of existence (and without doing violence to the constitutional intention of the Electoral College), but this would not lessen the contemporary hostility to it as undemocratic. It is to the main problem of democracy and the Electoral College that we may now turn. But we may do so, after this historical inquiry into the purpose of the electors, emancipated from the prejudice that regards the Electoral College as having originated in an archaic, undemocratic intention.

An "Undemocratic" System?

The gravamen of the "undemocratic" indictment of the Electoral College rests on the possibility that, because votes are aggregated within the states by the general-ticket system in which the winner takes all, a loser in the national popular vote may nonetheless become president by winning a majority of the electoral votes of the states. This is supposedly the "loaded pistol" to our heads, our quadrennial game of Russian roulette; indeed, no terms seem lurid enough to express the contemporary horror at this possibility. This is what shocks our modern democratic sensibilities and, once the issue is permitted to be stated in this way, it takes a very brave man or woman to defend the Electoral College. But, fortunately, courage is not required; it suffices to reformulate the issue and get it on its proper footing.

In fact, presidential elections are already just about as democratic as they can be. We already have one-man, one-vote—*but in the states*. Elections are as freely and democratically contested as elections can be—*but in the states*. Victory always goes democratically to the winner of the raw popular vote—*but in the states*. The label given to the proposed reform, "direct popular election," is a misnomer; the elections have already become as directly popular as they can be—*but in the states*. Despite all their democratic rhetoric, the reformers do not propose to make our presidential elections more directly democratic; they only propose to make them more directly *national*, by entirely removing the states from the electoral process. Democracy thus is not the question regarding the Electoral College, federalism is: should our presidential elections remain in part *federally* democratic, or should we make them completely *nationally* democratic?

Whatever we decide, then, democracy itself is not at stake in our decision, only the prudential question of how to channel and organize the popular will. That makes everything easier. When the question is only whether the federally democratic aspect of the Electoral College should be abandoned in order to prevent the remotely possible election of a president who had not won the national popular vote, it does not seem so hard to opt for retaining some federalism in this homogenizing, centralizing age. When federalism has already been weakened, perhaps inevitably in modern circumstances, why further weaken the federal elements in our political system by destroying the informal federal element that has historically evolved in our system of presidential elections?

The crucial general-ticket system, adopted in the 1830s for reasons pertinent then, has become in our time a constitutionally unplanned but vital support for federalism. Also called the "unit rule" system, it provides that the state's entire electoral vote goes to the winner of the popular vote in the state. Resting entirely on the voluntary legislative action of each state, this informal historical development, combined with the formal constitutional provision, has generated a federal element in the Electoral College which sends a federalizing impulse throughout our whole political process. It makes the states as states dramatically and pervasively important in the whole presidential selection process, from the earliest strategies in the nominating campaign, through the convention and final election. Defederalize the presidential election—which is what direct popular election boils down to—and a contrary nationalizing impulse will gradually work its way throughout the political process. The nominating process naturally takes its cues from the electing process; were the president to be elected in a single national election, the same cuing process would continue, but in reverse.[8]

It is hard to think of a worse time than the present, when so much already tends toward excessive centralization, to strike an unnecessary blow at the federal quality of our political order. The federal aspect of the electoral controversy has received inadequate attention; indeed, it is regarded by many as irrelevant to it. The argument has been that the president is the representative of "all the people" and, hence, that he should be elected by them in a wholly national way, unimpeded by the interposition of the states. Unfortunately, the prevailing conception of federalism encourages this erroneous view. We tend nowadays to have a narrowed conception of federalism, limiting it to the reserved powers of the states. But by focusing exclusively on the division of power between the states and the central government, we overlook an equally vital aspect of federalism: namely, the federal elements in the central government itself. The Senate (which, after all, helps make laws for all the people) is the most obvious example; it is organized on the federal principle of equal representation of each state. Even the House of Representatives has federal elements in its design and mode of operation. There is no reason, then, why the president, admittedly the representative of all of us, cannot represent us and hence be elected by us in a way corresponding to our compoundly federal and national character. The ABA Report, for example, begs the question when it says that "it seems most appropriate that the election of the nation's only two national officers be by national referendum."[9] They are our two *central* officers. But they are not our two *national* officers; under the Constitution, they are our two *partly federal, partly national* officers. Why should we wish to change them into our two *wholly* national officers?

Since democracy as such is not implicated in our choice—but only whether to choose our presidents in a partly federally democratic or a wholly national democratic way—we are perfectly free prudentially to choose the partly federal rather than the wholly national route. We need only strip away from the Electoral College reformers their democratic rhetorical dress in order to make the sensible choice with good conscience.

Our consciences will be further eased when we note that the abhorrence of the federal aspect of the Electoral College—which causes the potential discrepancy between electoral and popular votes—cannot logically be limited to the Electoral College. It rests upon premises that necessitate abhorrence of any and all *district* forms of election. What is complained about in the Electoral College is endemic to all districted electoral systems, whether composed of states, or congressional districts, or parliamentary constituencies. If population is not exactly evenly distributed in all the districts (and it never can be), both in sheer numbers and in their political predispositions, then the possibility cannot be removed that the winner of a majority of the districts may not also be the winner of the raw popular vote. Regarding the British Parliament and the American Congress, for example, this is not merely a speculative matter or something that has not happened since 1888 (when Cleveland narrowly won the popular vote but lost the electoral vote, and thus the presidency, to Harrison), as in the case of the American presidency. It has happened more often and far more recently in England, where popular-minority governments are as possible as popular-minority presidents are here.[10] It is a source of wonder that Electoral College critics, who are often partisans of the parliamentary system, regard with equanimity in that system what they cannot abide in the American case. There the whole power of government, both legislative and executive, is at stake in an election, while here only the executive power is involved.

And not only can and does the national popular-vote–district-vote discrepancy occur in England, it can and does occur here regarding control of both the House and the Senate. Why is it not a loaded pistol to our democratic heads when control over our lawmaking bodies can fall, and has fallen, into the hands of the party that lost in the national popular vote?[11] Have we come to view control of the presidency as so much more important than control of the House or Senate that we regard the discrepancy with horror in the one case and practically ignore it in the other? Granting the differences between electing a single chief executive and a numerous legislature, still the logic of the attack on the Electoral College also impugns the districted basis of both houses of Congress. The Senate has in fact been attacked on just that basis. Not only are popular votes for the Senate federally aggregated on a state basis, but also each state has an equal number of seats despite population inequalities; therefore, a discrepancy between the national popular vote and control of the Senate is likely to occur more often and more grossly than in the case of the presidency. Now just as the president is the president of all of the people, so too does the Senate make law and policy for the whole people, as we have noted. But we accept the districted basis of the Senate despite its "undemocratic" potential, partly because of its nearly sacrosanct constitutional status, and also because we see the wisdom of departing, in this instance, from strict national majoritarianism.

The House has largely escaped the "undemocratic" charge (especially now, after major reapportionment) despite the fact that its districted basis likewise creates a potential discrepancy between winning a majority of seats and winning the national popular vote for Congress. By the populistic reasoning and rhetoric that attacks the Electoral College, the House also fails the standard of national majoritarianism. But we quite ungrudgingly see the wisdom in departing from that standard in order to secure the many advantages of local districting. To indicate only a few: First, there is democratic responsiveness to local needs, interests, and opinions in general. Americans have always believed that there is more to democracy itself than merely maximizing national majoritarianism; our idea of democracy includes responsiveness to *local* majorities as well. Further, because of our multiplicity of interests, ethnic groups, religions, and races, we have always believed in local democratic responsiveness to geographically based minorities whose interests may otherwise be utterly neglected; such minorities secure vigorous direct representation, for example, only because of the districted basis of the House of Representatives. The state-by-state responsiveness of the Electoral College is an equally legitimate form of districted, local democratic responsiveness. There is also the security to liberty that results from the districted decentralization of the political basis of the legislature; and we cherish also the multiplication of opportunities for voluntary political participation that likewise results from that districted decentralization. Finally, we cherish the guarantee that districting provides, that power in the legislature will be nationally distributed, rather than concentrated in regional majorities, as would be possible in a nondistricted election of the House. In short, in the case of both the House and the Senate, we accept the risk (and the occasional reality) of the national popular-vote–district-vote discrepancy because the advantages to be gained are great and because the House and Senate remain nationally democratic enough to satisfy any reasonable standard of democracy.

This kind of complex reasoning is the hallmark of the American idea of democracy: a taking into account of local as well as national democratic considerations and, even more importantly, blending democratic considerations with all the other things that contribute to political well-being. What is so disturbing about the attack on the Electoral College is the way the reasoning and the rhetoric of the reformers depart from this traditional American posture toward democracy. They scant or simply ignore all the other considerations and put the presidential election process to the single test of national democratic numbers. In contrast, the fundamental premise of the traditional American idea of democracy is that democracy, like all other forms of government, cannot be the be-all and end-all, the political *summum bonum;* rather, the political system must be made democratic enough and then structured, channeled, and moderated, so that on a democratic basis *all* the democratic considerations (in addition to the purely numerical) and all the other vital political considerations can be attended to.

The issue regarding the Electoral College, then, is not democratic reform versus the retention of an undemocratic system but rather a matter of which kind of democratic reasoning is to prevail in presidential elections—the traditional American idea that channels and constrains democracy or a rival idea that wishes democracy to be its entirely untrammeled and undifferentiated national self.

One more point may usefully be made regarding the charge that the Electoral College is undemocratic. I have already argued that our presidential elections under the Electoral College are thoroughly democratic, albeit partly federally democratic, and that democracy may profitably be blended with the advantages of districting. But even on the basis of purely national democratic terms, the potential popular-vote–electoral-vote discrepancy of the Electoral College may be tolerated with good democratic conscience.

Not only has the discrepancy not occurred for nearly a century, but no one even suggests that it is ever likely to occur save by a very small margin. The margin in the last actual occurrence, in 1888, was of minute proportions; and the imaginary "near misses"—those horrendous hypotheticals—are always in the range of zero to one-tenth of 1 percent.[12] The great undemocratic threat of the Electoral College, then, is the possibility that, so to speak, of 80 million votes, 50 percent minus one would rule over 50 percent plus one. Now there really is something strange in escalating this popgun possibility into a loaded pistol. For one thing, the statistical margin of error in the vote count (let alone other kinds of errors and chance circumstances) is larger than any anticipated discrepancy; that is to say, the discrepancy might be only apparent and not real. But even granting the possibility that 50 percent minus one might prevail over 50 percent plus one, how undemocratic would that really be? The answer is suggested by the fact that, in the long history of democratic thought, the problem never even arose before the present, let alone troubled anyone. It took us to invent it. When we understand why, we will also see that it is a spurious problem or, at least, a trivial one.

Historically, the problem of democracy was not about minute margins of electoral victory, but about whether, say, 5 percent (the rich and wellborn few), should rule over 95 percent (the poor many), to use the classical terms. That is what the real struggles of democracy were all about. Only a severe case of doctrinaire myopia blinds us to that and makes us see, instead, a crisis in the mathematical niceties of elections where no fundamental democratic issues are involved. Democracy is not at stake in our elections, only the decision as to which shifting portion of an overall democratic electorate will temporarily capture executive office. What serious difference does it make to any fundamental democratic value if, in such elections, 50 percent minus one of the voters *might—very* infrequently— win the presidency from 50 percent plus one of the voters? Only a country as thoroughly and safely democratic as ours could invent the 50 percent problem and make a tempest in a democratic teapot out of it.

The irrelevance of the potential popular-vote–electoral-vote discrepancy to any important democratic value is illustrated if we consider the following question: Would the Electoral College reformers really regard it as a disaster for democracy if Franklin D. Roosevelt (or any liberal Democrat) had beaten Herbert Hoover (or any conservative Republican) in the electoral vote but had lost by a handful in the national popular vote? The question is not meant, of course, in any spirit of partisan twitting. Rather, it is intended to suggest that no sensible person could seriously regard it as a disaster for democracy if—to use the language of caricature—a coalition of the poor, of labor, of blacks, et al., had thus squeaked by a coalition of the rich, the powerful, the privileged, and the like. To point this out is not to depreciate the importance of such an electoral outcome for the course of public policy. It is only to deny that it would threaten or make a mockery of the democratic foundations of our political order. To think that it would is to ignore the relevant socioeconomic requisites of democracy, and to be panicked into wide-reaching constitutional revisions by the bogeyman of the 50 percent minus one possibility. To risk such revision for such a reason is to reduce democracy not only to a matter of mere numbers, but to minute numbers, and to abstract numbers, drained of all socioeconomic significance for democracy.[13]

A "Complex" System?

The ABA Report does not make clear what is "complex" about the Electoral College or why complexity as such is bad. Perhaps the fear is that voters are baffled by the complexity of the Electoral College and that their bafflement violates a democratic norm. It must be admitted that an opinion survey could easily be devised that shows the average voter to be shockingly ignorant of what the Electoral College is and how it operates. But then opinion surveys almost always show the average voter to be shockingly ignorant of whatever a survey happens to be asking him about. It all depends upon what kind of knowledge the voter is expected to have. I would argue that most voters have a solid working knowledge of what a presidential election is all about. They know that they are voting for the candidate of their choice and that the candidate with the most votes wins in their state. And when watching the results on television or reading about them in the papers, they surely discover how the election came out. However ignorant they may be of the details of the Electoral College, their ignorance does not seem to affect at all the intention and meaning of their vote, or their acceptance of the electoral outcome. What more is necessary than that? What is the use of making the process less complex?

However, the animus against the complexity of the Electoral College surely goes deeper than a fear that voters are unable to explain it when asked. There seems to be a hostility to complexity as such. This hostility has a long history. It goes back at least to those French Enlightenment thinkers who scolded John Adams for the unnecessary complexity, for example, of American bicameralism. However such complexity had helped to mitigate monarchical severities, of what possible use could bicameralism be, they asked, now that America had established popular government? When the people rule, they insisted, one branch is quite enough; no complexity should stand in the way of straightforwardly recording and carrying out the popular will. The answer to them, and to all like-minded democratic simplifiers ever since, derives from the very essence of American democracy, which is precisely to be complex. The American idea of democracy, as argued above, is to take into account both local and national considerations, and also to moderate democracy and blend it with as many other things as are necessary to the public good. That blending necessitates complexity.

The Electoral College is, of course, only one example of the complexity that characterizes our entire political system. Bicameralism is complex; federalism is complex; judicial review is complex; the suspensory executive veto is a complex arrangement; the Bill of Rights introduces a thousand complexities. Are these also to be faulted on grounds of complexity? If a kind of prissy intelligibility is to be made the standard for deciding what should remain and what should be simplified in American government, how much would be left in place? In all fairness, the question is not whether our political system or any part of it is complex, but whether there is a good reason for any particular complexity. The skeptical, self-doubting American idea of democracy does not assume that the rich complexity of democratic reality is exhausted by mere national majoritarianism, nor does it assume that all good things automatically flow from democracy. It therefore asks of any institution not only whether it is democratic, but also whether, while leaving the system democratic enough, it contributes to fulfilling the complex requirements of democracy and to securing some worthwhile purpose not secured simply by democracy itself. That is the only appropriate question regarding the complexity of the Electoral College.

Some of the affirmative answers to that question as regards our electoral institution—especially the federal element blended into our democracy by the historical development of the Electoral College—have already been suggested. Others will more conveniently come up under two of the remaining headings of the ABA Report's indictment against the Electoral College.[14] To these we may now proceed.

An "Ambiguous" System?

This charge is rather puzzling. It is so far off the mark that a rebuttal is hardly required; rather, it supplies the opportunity to point out a particular advantage of the Electoral College in comparison with its proposed substitute. Far from speaking unclearly or confusingly, the Electoral College has delivered exceptionally prompt and unequivocal electoral pronouncements. This is not to say that there have never been any delays or uncertainties. Whenever an election is closely divided, as ours often have been and are likely to be, no election system can deliver prompt and absolutely certain verdicts, free of the ambiguity that inheres in the electorate's own behavior. But when a realistic rather than a utopian standard is applied, the Electoral College has to be rated an unqualified success. To deny this betrays a reluctance to credit the Electoral College with any merit at all. Or perhaps it is another instance of the human propensity, remarked on by Hobbes, to attribute all inconveniences to the particular form of government under which one lives, rather than to recognize that some inconveniences are intrinsic to government as such regardless of its form.[15] This propensity seems to explain the finding of ambiguity in the way the present system works.

To judge fairly the charge of ambiguity, then, the Electoral College must be compared in this regard with other electoral systems, and especially with the 40 percent plus–runoff system proposed by President Carter and Senator Bayh as its replacement. Under the proposed system, the nation forms a single electoral district; the candidate who gets the most popular votes wins, provided the winning total equals at least 40 percent of the total number of votes cast; failing that, there would be a runoff election between the two candidates who had the most votes. Let us consider the prospects for ambiguity under this proposed system, in comparison with the actual experience under the Electoral College.

The American electorate has a fundamental tendency to divide closely, with "photo finish" elections being almost the rule rather than the exception. The Electoral College almost always announces these close election outcomes with useful amplification. In purely numerical popular votes, an election outcome might be uncertain and vulnerable to challenge; but the Electoral College replaces the numerical uncertainty with an unambiguously visible constitutional majority that sustains the legitimacy of the electoral result. If this magnifying lens is removed, the "squeaker" aspect of our presidential elections will become more visible and, probably, much more troubling. For example, the problem of error and fraud, no doubt endemic in some degree to all electoral systems, could very well be aggravated under the proposed national system, because every single precinct polling place could come under bitter scrutiny as relevant to a close and disputed national outcome. In contrast, under the Electoral College, ambiguity of outcome sufficient even to warrant challenge is infrequent and is always limited to but a few states. Indeed, the massive and undeniable fact is that, for a whole century, the Electoral College has produced unambiguous outcomes in every single presidential election, accepted by the losing candidate and party and by the whole American people with unfaltering legitimacy.[16]

Not only is it extremely unlikely that the proposed replacement could match this record of unambiguity, but the 40 percent plus plurality provision could very well introduce a different and graver kind of ambiguity into our political system. This would not be uncertainty as to who is the winner, but a profounder uncertainty as to whether the winner is truly the choice of the American people. Under the modern Electoral College, we have elected popular-majority presidents about half the time, and plurality presidents with close to 50 percent of the vote the rest of the time, save for three who received less than 45 percent of the popular vote. This is a remarkable record of unambiguity in regard to public support compared with the history of most other democratic systems. But given the dynamics of American political behavior, the proposed 40 percent plus plurality provision might very well *typically* produce winners at or just above the 40 percent level.

The Electoral College strongly encourages the two-party system by almost always narrowing the election to a race between the two major-party candidates. Obviously, when there are only two serious competitors, the winner usually has a majority or large plurality of the total vote cast. But as we shall shortly see, the new system would encourage minor and maverick candidacies. This multiplication of competitors would likely reduce the winning margin to the bare 40 percent plurality requirement of the new system. If so, we would have traded in a majority- or high plurality-presidency for one in which nearly 60 percent of the people might often have voted against the incumbent. How ironic it would be if a reform demanded in the name of democracy and majority rule resulted in a permanent minority presidency!

A "Dangerous" System?

"Dangers" of the Electoral College. It is not possible here to discuss all the dangers that alarm critics of the Electoral College—for example, the faithless electors, or a cabal of them,[17] or the problem of the contingency election in the House of Representatives. Some pose real enough problems and would have to be dealt with in a fuller discussion. But the present remarks are limited to the main danger that the reformers fear; namely, the popular-vote–electoral-vote discrepancy. This is the loaded pistol pointed to our heads, the threat that necessitates radical constitutional revision. Now the funny thing about this loaded pistol is that the last time it went off, in 1888, no one got hurt; no one even hollered. As far as I can tell, there was hardly a ripple of constitutional discontent, not a trace of dangerous delegitimation, and nothing remotely resembling the crisis predicted by present-day critics of the Electoral College. But it must be sadly acknowledged that the next time it happens there might well be far greater public distress. It would be due in large part to the decades of populistic denunciation of the Electoral College; a kind of self-confirming prophecy would be at work.

All that is needed to defuse this danger is for the undermining of the moral authority of the Electoral College to cease. The American people will not, on their own initiative, react with rage if one of the near-misses actually occurs. As after 1888, they will go about their business and, perhaps, straighten things out in the next election, as when they elected Cleveland in 1892. They will go about their business as they did in a parallel instance, after Vice President Agnew's resignation and Watergate, when the provisions of the Twenty-fifth Amendment went doubly into effect. The democratic foundations of our political system, and even the vigor of the presidency, were not weakened by the temporary absence of the majority or plurality popular support that normally undergirds the presidency. There need be no dangerous weakening should the Electoral College again produce a temporary shortfall in popular support—if only the reformers cease to cry havoc, and if those who ought to speak up do so and help the American people learn to enjoy the compatibility of the Electoral College with the American idea of democracy.

Dangers of Direct Election. Not every danger alleged to inhere in our present electoral system could thus be made to evaporate merely by the exercise of our own common sense; like every political institution, the Electoral College contains dangerous possibilities. But this much may be said about them: all the dangers critics claim to see in the Electoral College are entirely matters of speculation. Some have never actually occurred, and others have not occurred for nearly a century. Nothing whatever has actually gone wrong with the Electoral College for a very long time. Experience has demonstrated that the dangers incident to the present system are neither grave nor likely to occur. But what of the dangers incident to the proposed reform? It is as important to speculate about them as to frighten ourselves with imaginary possibilities under the Electoral College. Three dangers seem seriously to threaten under the proposed reform: weakening the two-party system, weakening party politics generally, and further imperializing the presidency.

Many have warned that the 40 percent plus–runoff system would encourage minor parties and in time undermine the two-party system. The encouragement consists in the runoff provision of the proposed reform, that is, in the possibility that minor parties will get enough votes in the first election to force a runoff. Supporters of the proposed change deny this likelihood. For example, the ABA Report argues that a third party is unlikely to get the 20 percent of the popular vote necessary to force a runoff. Perhaps so, and this has been very reassuring to supporters of the reform. But why does it have to be just "a" third party? Why cannot the runoff be forced by the combined votes of a half dozen or more minor parties that enter the first election? Indeed, they are all there waiting in the wings. The most powerful single constraint on minor-party presidential candidacies has always been the "don't throw your vote away" fear that caused their support to melt as election day approached. Norman Thomas, who knew this better than anyone, was certain that a national popular election of the kind now proposed would have immensely improved the Socialist electoral results. Now this is not to say that the Electoral College alone is what prevents ideological parties like that of the Socialists from winning elections in America. Obviously, other and more powerful factors ultimately determine that. But what the electoral machinery can determine is whether such parties remain electorally irrelevant, minuscule failures, or whether they can achieve sufficient electoral success to fragment the present two-party system. The relevant question is not whether the proposed reform of the Electoral College would radically change the ideological complexion of American parties, but whether it would multiply their number.

Moreover, not only ideological parties would be encouraged by the proposed change, but also minor parties and minor candidacies of all sorts. Sectional third parties would not be weakened by the 40 percent plus–runoff arrangement; they would retain their sectional appeal and pick up additional votes all over the country. The threat that dissident wings might bolt from one of the two major parties would instantly become more credible and thereby more disruptive within them; sooner or later the habit of bolting would probably take hold. Would there not also be an inducement to militant wings of ethnic, racial, and religious groups to abandon the major party framework and go it alone? And, as the recent proliferation of primary candidacies suggests, would-be "charismatics" might frequently take their case to the general electorate, given the inducements of the proposed new machinery.[18]

All this might not happen immediately. The two-party habit is strong among us, and many factors would continue to give it strength. But the proposed reform of the Electoral College would remove or weaken what is generally regarded as the most powerful cause of the two-party system, namely, the presidency as a "single-member district." There would, of course, still be a single office finally to be won or lost, but *not in the first election*. That is the key. If runoffs become the rule, as is likely, the first election would become in effect a kind of two-member district. There would be two winners in it; we would have created a valuable new electoral prize—a second place finish in the preliminary election. This would be a boon to the strong minor candidacies; needing now only to seem a viable alternative for second place, they could more easily make a plausible case to potential supporters. But, more important, there would be something to win for nearly everyone in the first, or preliminary, election. Minor party votes now shrink away as the election nears and practically disappear on election day. As is well known, this is because minor-party supporters desert their preferred candidates to vote for the "lesser evil" of the major candidates. But the proposed reform would remove the reason to do so. On the contrary, as in multiparty parliamentary systems, the voter could vote with his heart because that would in fact also be the calculating thing to do. There would be plenty of time to vote for the lesser evil in the eventual runoff election. The trial heat would be the time to help the preferred minor party show its strength. Even a modest showing would enable the minor party to participate in the frenetic bargaining inevitably incident to runoff elections. And even a modest showing would establish a claim to the newly available public financing that would simultaneously be an inducement to run and a means to strengthen one's candidacy.

Let us examine an illustration of the difference under the two electoral systems. At present, opinion polls teach minor-party supporters to desert come election day; the voter sees that his party has no chance of winning and acts accordingly. Under the proposed system, the polls would give exactly the opposite signal: hold fast. The voter would see his party or candidate making a showing and would see that a runoff was guaranteed; he would have no reason to desert his party. The first election would, thus, cease to have the deterrent effect on minor parties; the prospect of the runoff would change everything. True, in such matters prediction is difficult. But it is clearly likely that the two-party system would be dangerously weakened by the proposed reform, whereas it is certain that it has been created and strengthened under the Electoral College. Most Americans agree that the two-party system is a valuable way of channeling democracy because that mode of democratic decision produces valuable qualities of moderation, consensus, and stability. It follows then that the proposed reform threatens a serious injury to the American political system.

Not only might the change weaken the two-party system, but it might well also have an enfeebling effect on party politics generally. The regular party politicians, which is to say, the state and local politicians, would become less important to presidential candidates. This tendency is already evident in the effect the presidential primaries are having; regular party machinery is becoming less important in the nominating process, and the individual apparatus of the candidates more important. The defederalizing of the presidential election seems likely to strengthen this tendency. No longer needing to carry states, the presidential candidates would find the regular politicians, who are most valuable for tipping the balance in a state, of diminishing importance for their freewheeling search for popular votes. They probably would rely more and more on direct-mail and media experts, and on purely personal coteries, in conducting campaigns that would rely primarily on the mass media. The consequence would seem to be to disengage the presidential campaign from the party machinery and from the states and to isolate the presidency from their moderating effect. If "merchandising" the president has become an increasingly dangerous tendency, nationalizing and plebiscitizing the presidency would seem calculated only to intensify the danger.

This raises, finally, the question of the effect of the proposed reform on the presidency as an institution, that is, on the "imperial presidency." The populistic rhetoric that denounces the Electoral College as undemocratic has had, since the time of the New Deal, a corollary inclination to inflate the importance of the presidency. In recent years, however, we have all learned to be cautious about the extent of presidential power. Yet the proposed change could only have an inflating effect on it. The presidency has always derived great moral authority and political power from the claim that the president is the only representative of all the people. Why increase the force of that claim by magnifying the national and plebiscitary foundations of the presidency? This would be to enhance the presidential claims at just the moment when so much fear had been expressed about the "imperial presidency."

Many who deal with the Electoral College are concerned chiefly with its consequences for partisan purposes. They support or oppose it because of its alleged tendency to push the presidency in a liberal direction. As for myself, I am not at all sure what those partisan effects used to be, are now, or will become in the future. Accordingly, it seems a good time to rise above party considerations to the level of constitutional principle. On that level, it seems quite clear to me that the effects of the proposed change are likely to be quite bad. And it likewise seems quite clear to me that the Electoral College is easy to defend, once one gets the hang of it. It is a paradigm of the American idea of democracy. Thus to defend it is not only to help retain a valuable part of our political system, but also to help rediscover what the American idea of democracy is.

PART THREE
Background Materials

Provisions in the Constitution for Presidential Selection

Article II

Section 1. The executive Power shall be vested in a President of the United States of America. He shall hold his Office during the Term of four Years, and, together with the Vice President, chosen for the same Term, be elected, as follows:

Each state shall appoint, in such Manner as the Legislature thereof may direct, a Number of Electors, equal to the whole Number of Senators and Representatives to which the State may be entitled in the Congress: but no Senator or Representative, or Person holding an Office of Trust or Profit under the United States, shall be appointed an Elector. . . .

The Twelfth Amendment
(Ratified June 15, 1804)

The Electors shall meet in their respective states and vote by ballot for President and Vice-President, one of whom, at least, shall not be an inhabitant of the same state with themselves; they shall name in their ballots the person voted for as President, and in distinct ballots the person voted for as Vice-President, and they shall make distinct lists of all persons voted for as President, and of all persons voted for as Vice-President, and of the number of votes for each, which lists they shall sign and certify, and transmit sealed to the seat of the government of the United

States, directed to the President of the Senate;—The President of the Senate shall, in the presence of the Senate and House of Representatives, open all the certificates and the votes shall then be counted;—The person having the greatest number of votes for President, shall be the President, if such number[1] be a majority of the whole number of Electors appointed; and if no person have such majority, then from the persons having the highest numbers not exceeding three on the list of those voted for as President, the House of Representatives shall choose immediately, by ballot, the President. But in choosing the President, the votes shall be taken by states, the representation from each state having one vote; a quorum for this purpose shall consist of a member or members from two-thirds of the states, and a majority of all the states shall be necessary to a choice. [And if the House of Representatives shall not choose a President whenever the right of choice shall devolve upon them, before the fourth day of March next following, then the Vice-President shall act as President, as in the case of the death or other constitutional disability of the President.][2]—The person having the greatest number of votes as Vice-President, shall the the Vice-President, if such number be a majority of the whole number of Electors appointed, and if no person have a majority, then from the two highest numbers on the list, the Senate shall choose the Vice-President; a quorum for the purpose shall consist of two-thirds of the whole number of Senators, and a majority of the whole number shall be necessary to a choice. But no person constitutionally ineligible to the office of President shall be eligible to that of Vice-President of the United States.

The Twentieth Amendment
(Ratified January 23, 1933)

SECTION 1. The terms of the President and Vice President shall end at noon on the 20th day of January, and the terms of Senators and Representatives at noon on the 3d day of January, of the years in which such terms would have ended if this article had not been ratified; and the terms of their successors shall then begin.

SECTION 2. The Congress shall assemble at least once in every year, and such meeting shall begin at noon on the 3d day of January, unless they shall by law appoint a different day.

SECTION 3. If, at the time fixed for the beginning of the term of the President, the President elect shall have died, the Vice President elect shall become President. If a President shall not have been chosen before the time fixed for the beginning of his term, or if the President elect shall have failed to qualify, then the Vice President elect shall act as President until a President shall have qualified; and the Congress may by law provide for the case wherein neither a President elect nor a Vice President elect shall have qualified, declaring who shall then act as President, or the manner in which one who is to act shall be selected, and such person shall act accordingly until a President or Vice President shall have qualified.

SECTION 4. The Congress may by law provide for the case of the death of any of the persons from whom the House of Representatives may choose a President whenever the right of choice shall have devolved upon them, and for the case of the death of any of the persons from whom the Senate may choose a Vice President whenever the right of choice shall have devolved upon them. . . .

The Twenty-third Amendment
(Ratified March 29, 1961)

SECTION 1. The District constituting the seat of Government of the United States shall appoint in such manner as the Congress may direct: A number of electors of President and Vice President equal to the whole number of Senators and Representatives in Congress to which the District would be entitled if it were a State, but in no event more than the least populous State; they shall be in addition to those appointed by the States, but they shall be considered, for the purposes of the election of President and Vice President, to be electors appointed by a State; and they shall meet in the District and perform such duties as provided by the twelfth article of amendment. . . .

APPENDIX B

Statutory Provisions for Presidential Selection

The following provisions are to be found in title 3, chapter 1, of the United States Code (11th edition), a consolidation and codification of all the general and permanent laws of the United States in force on January 3, 1989. The code consists of eighteen volumes (plus an index in seven volumes), and is divided into fifty "titles," organized by subject matter. Thus, title 3 is entitled "The President," and its chapter 1, "Presidential Elections and Vacancies."

1. Time of appointing electors

The electors of President and Vice President shall be appointed, in each State, on the Tuesday next after the first Monday in November, in every fourth year succeeding every election of a President and Vice President.

2. Failure to make choice on prescribed day

Whenever any State has held an election for the purpose of choosing electors, and has failed to make a choice on the day prescribed by law, the electors may be appointed on a subsequent day in such a manner as the legislature of such State may direct.

3. Number of electors

The number of electors shall be equal to the number of Senators and Representatives to which the several States are by law entitled at the time when the President and Vice President to be chosen come into office; except, that where no apportionment of Representatives has been made after any enumeration, at the time of choosing electors, the number of electors shall be according to the then existing apportionment of Senators and Representatives.

4. Vacancies in electoral college

Each State may, by law, provide for the filling of any vacancies which may occur in its college of electors when such college meets to give its electoral vote.

5. Determination of controversy as to appointment of electors

If any State shall have provided, by laws enacted prior to the day fixed for the appointment of the electors, for its final determination of any controversy or contest concerning the appointment of all or any of the electors of such State, by judicial or other methods or procedures, and such determination shall have been made at least six days before the time fixed for the meeting of the electors, such determination made pursuant to such law so existing on said day, and made at least six days prior to said time of meeting of the electors, shall be conclusive, and shall govern in the counting of the electoral votes as provided in the Constitution, and as hereinafter regulated, so far as the ascertainment of the electors appointed by such State is concerned.

6. Credentials of electors; transmission to Archivist of the United States and to Congress; public inspection

It shall be the duty of the executive of each State, as soon as practicable after the conclusion of the appointment of the electors in such State by the final ascertainment, under and in pursuance of the laws of such State providing for such ascertainment, to communicate by registered mail under the seal of the State to the Archivist of the United States a certificate of such ascertainment of the electors appointed, setting forth the names of such electors and the canvass or other ascertainment under the laws of such State of the number of votes given or cast for each person for whose appointment any and all votes have been given or cast; and it shall also thereupon be the duty of the executive of each State to deliver to the electors of such State, on or before the day on which they are required by section 7 of this title to meet, six duplicate-originals of the same certificate under the seal of the State; and if there shall have been any final determination in a State in the manner provided for by law of a controversy or contest concerning the appointment of all or any of the electors of such State, it shall be the duty of the executive of such State, as soon as practicable after such determination, to communicate under the seal of the State to the Archivist of the United States a certificate of such determination in form and manner as the same shall have been made; and the certificate or certificates so received by the Archivist of the United States shall be preserved by him for one year and shall be a part of the public records of his office and shall be open to public inspection; and the Archivist of the United States at the first meeting of Congress thereafter shall transmit to the two Houses of Congress copies in full of each and every such certificate so received at the National Archives and Records Administration.

7. Meeting and vote of electors

The electors of President and Vice President of each State shall meet and give their votes on the first Monday after the second Wednesday in December next following their appointment at such place in each State as the legislature of such State shall direct.

8. Manner of voting

The electors shall vote for President and Vice President, respectively, in the manner directed by the Constitution.

9. Certificates of votes for President and Vice President

The electors shall make and sign six certificates of all the votes given by them, each of which certificates shall contain two distinct lists, one of the votes for President and the other of the votes for Vice President, and shall annex to each of the certificates one of the lists of the electors which shall have been furnished to them by direction of the executive of the State.

10. Sealing and endorsing certificates

The electors shall seal up the certificates so made by them, and certify upon each that the lists of all the votes of such State given for President, and of all the votes given for Vice President, are contained therein.

11. Disposition of certificates

The electors shall dispose of the certificates so made by them and the lists attached thereto in the following manner:

First. They shall forthwith forward by registered mail one of the same to the President of the Senate at the seat of government.

Second. Two of the same shall be delivered to the secretary of state of the State, one of which shall be held subject to the order of the President of the Senate, the other to be preserved by him for one year and shall be a part of the public records of his office and shall be open to public inspection.

Third. On the day thereafter they shall forward by registered mail two of such certificates and lists to the Archivist of the United States at the seat of government, one of which shall be held subject to the order of the President of the Senate. The other shall be preserved by the Archivist of the United States for one year and shall be a part of the public records of his office and shall be open to public inspection.

Fourth. They shall forthwith cause the other of the certificates and lists to be delivered to the judge of the district in which the electors shall have assembled.

12. Failure of certificates of electors to reach President of Senate or Archivist of the United States; demand on State for certificate

When no certificate of vote and list mentioned in sections 9 and 11 of this title from any State shall have been received by the President of the Senate or by the Archivist of the United States by the fourth Wednesday in December, after the meeting of the electors shall have been held, the President of the Senate or, if he be absent from the seat of government, the Archivist of the United States shall request, by the most expeditious method available, the secretary of state of the State to send up the certificate and list lodged with him by the electors of such State; and it shall be his duty upon receipt of such request immediately to transmit same by registered mail to the President of the Senate at the seat of government.

13. Same; demand on district judge for certificate

When no certificates of votes from any State shall have been received at the seat of government on the fourth Wednesday in December, after the meeting of the electors shall have been held, the President of the Senate or, if he be absent from the seat of government, the Archivist of the United States shall send a special messenger to the district judge in whose custody one certificate of votes from that State has been lodged, and such judge shall forthwith transmit that list by the hand of such messenger to the seat of government.

14. Forfeiture for messenger's neglect of duty

Every person who, having been appointed, pursuant to section 13 of this title, to deliver the certificates of the votes of the electors to the President of the Senate, and having accepted such appointment, shall neglect to perform the services required from him, shall forfeit the sum of $1,000.

15. Counting electoral votes in Congress

Congress shall be in session on the sixth day of January succeeding every meeting of the electors. The Senate and House of Representatives shall meet in the Hall of the House of Representatives at the hour of 1 o'clock in the afternoon on that day, and the President of the Senate shall be their presiding officer. Two tellers shall be previously appointed on the part of the Senate and two on the part of the House of Representatives, to whom shall be handed, as they are opened by the President of the Senate, all the certificates and papers purporting to be certificates of the electoral votes, which certificates and papers shall be opened, presented, and acted upon in the alphabetical order of the States, beginning with the letter A; and said tellers, having then read the same in the presence and hearing of the two Houses, shall make a list of the votes as they shall appear from the said certificates; and the votes having been ascertained and counted according to the rules in this subchapter provided, the result of the same shall be delivered to the President of the Senate, who shall thereupon announce the state of the vote, which announcement shall be deemed a sufficient declaration of the persons, if any, elected President and Vice President of the United States, and, together with a list of the votes, be entered on the Journals of the two Houses. Upon such reading of any such certificate or paper, the President of the Senate shall call for objections, if any. Every objection shall be made in writing, and shall state clearly and concisely, and without argument, the ground thereof, and shall be signed by at least one Senator and one Member of the House of Representatives before the same shall be received. When all objections so made to any vote or paper from a State shall have been received and read, the Senate shall thereupon withdraw, and such objections shall be submitted to the Senate for its decision; and the Speaker of the House of Representatives shall, in like manner, submit such objections to the House of Representatives for its decision; and no electoral vote or votes from any State which shall have been regularly given by electors whose appointment has been lawfully certified to according to section 6 of this title from which but one return has been received shall be rejected, but the two Houses concurrently may reject the vote or votes when they agree that such vote or votes have not been so regularly given by electors whose appointment has been so certified. If more than one return or paper purporting to be a return from a State shall have been received by the President of the Senate, those votes, and those only, shall be counted which shall have been regularly given by the electors who are shown by the determination mentioned in section 5 of this title to have been appointed, if the determination in said section provided for shall have been made, or by such successors or substitutes, in case of a vacancy in the board of electors so ascertained, as have been appointed to fill such vacancy in the mode provided by the laws of the State; but in case there shall arise the question which of two or more of such State authorities determining what electors have been appointed, as mentioned in section 5 of this title, is the lawful tribunal of such State, the votes regularly given of those electors, and those only, of such State shall be counted whose title as electors the two Houses, acting separately, shall concurrently decide is supported by the decision of such State so authorized by its law; and in such case of more than one return or paper purporting to be a return from a State, if there shall have been no such determination of the question in the State aforesaid, then those votes, and those only, shall be counted which the two Houses shall concurrently decide were cast by lawful electors appointed in accordance with the laws of the State, unless the two Houses, acting separately, shall concurrently decide such votes not to be the lawful votes of the legally appointed electors of such State. But if the two Houses shall disagree in respect of the counting of such votes, then, and in that case, the votes of the electors whose appointment shall have been certified by the executive of the State, under the seal thereof, shall be counted. When the two Houses have voted, they shall immediately again meet, and the presiding officer shall then announce the decision of the questions submitted. No votes or papers from any other State shall be acted upon until the objections previously made to the votes or papers from any State shall have been finally disposed of.

16. Same; seats for officers and members of two houses in joint meeting

At such joint meeting of the two Houses seats shall be provided as follows: For the President of the Senate, the Speaker's chair; for the Speaker, immediately upon his left; the Senators, in the body of the Hall upon the right of the presiding officer; for the Representatives, in the body of the Hall not provided for the Senators; for the tellers, Secretary of the Senate, and Clerk of the House of Representatives, at the Clerk's desk; for the other officers of the two Houses, in front of the Clerk's desk and upon each side of the Speaker's platform. Such joint meeting shall not be dissolved until the count of electoral votes shall be completed and the result declared; and no recess shall be taken unless a question shall have arisen in regard to counting any such votes, or otherwise under this subchapter, in which case it shall be competent for either House, acting separately, in the manner hereinbefore provided, to direct a recess of such House not beyond the next calendar day, Sunday excepted, at the hour of 10 o'clock in the forenoon. But if the counting of the electoral votes and the declaration of the result shall not have been completed before the fifth calendar day next after such first meeting of the two Houses, no further or other recess shall be taken by either House.

17. Same; limit of debate in each house

When the two Houses separate to decide upon an objection that may have been made to the counting of any electoral vote or votes from any State, or other question arising in the matter, each Senator and Representative may speak to such objection or question five minutes, and not more than once; but after such debate shall have lasted two hours it shall be the duty of the presiding officer of each House to put the main question without further debate.

18. Same; parliamentary procedure at joint meeting

While the two Houses shall be in meeting as provided

in this chapter, the President of the Senate shall have power to preserve order; and no debate shall be allowed and no question shall be put by the presiding officer except to either House on a motion to withdraw.

19. Vacancy in offices of both President and Vice President; officers eligible to act

(a) (1) If, by reason of death, resignation, removal from office, inability, or failure to qualify, there is neither a President nor Vice President to discharge the powers and duties of the office of President, then the Speaker of the House of Representatives shall, upon his resignation as Speaker and as Representative in Congress, act as President.

(2) The same rule shall apply in the case of the death, resignation, removal from office, or inability of an individual acting as President under this subsection.

(b) If, at the time when under subsection (a) of this section a Speaker is to begin the discharge of the powers and duties of the office of President, there is no Speaker, or the Speaker fails to qualify as Acting President, then the President pro tempore of the Senate shall, upon his resignation as President pro tempore and as Senator, act as President.

(c) An individual acting as President under subsection (a) or subsection (b) of this section shall continue to act until the expiration of the then current Presidential term, except that—

(1) if his discharge of the powers and duties of the office is founded in whole or in part on the failure of both the President-elect and the Vice President-elect to qualify, then he shall act only until a President or Vice President qualifies; and

(2) if his discharge of the powers and duties of the office is founded in whole or in part on the inability of the President or Vice President, then he shall act only until the removal of the disability of one of such individuals.

(d) (1) If, by reason of death, resignation, removal from office, inability, or failure to qualify, there is no President pro tempore to act as President under subsection (b) of this section, then the officer of the United States who is highest on the following list, and who is not under disability to discharge the powers and duties of the office of President shall act as President: Secretary of State, Secretary of the Treasury, Secretary of Defense, Attorney General, Secretary of the Interior, Secretary of Agriculture, Secretary of Commerce, Secretary of Labor, Secretary of Health and Human Services, Secretary of Housing and Urban Development, Secretary of Transportation, Secretary of Energy, Secretary of Education, Secretary of Veterans Affairs.

(2) An individual acting as President under this subsection shall continue so to do until the expiration of the then current Presidential term, but not after a qualified and prior-entitled individual is able to act, except that the removal of the disability of an individual higher on the list contained in paragraph (1) of this subsection or the ability to qualify on the part of an individual higher on such list shall not terminate his service.

(3) The taking of the oath of office by an individual specified in the list in paragraph (1) of this subsection shall be held to constitute his resignation from the office by virtue of the holding of which he qualifies to act as President.

(e) Subsections (a), (b), and (d) of this section shall apply only to such officers as are eligible to the office of President under the Constitution. Subsection (d) of this section shall apply only to officers appointed, by and with the advice and consent of the Senate, prior to the time of the death, resignation, removal from office, inability, or failure to qualify of the President pro tempore, and only to officers not under impeachment by the House of Representatives at the time the powers and duties of the office of President devolve upon them.

(f) During the period that any individual acts as President under this section, his compensation shall be at the rate then provided by law in the case of the President.

20. Resignation or refusal of office

The only evidence of a refusal to accept, or of a resignation of the office of President or Vice President, shall be an instrument in writing, declaring the same, and subscribed by the person refusing to accept or resigning, as the case may be, and delivered into the office of the Secretary of State.

Nomination and Binding of Presidential Electors

State	Candidates for Elector Are Nominated by PO: Party option CN: Party convention CO: Party committee	Are Electors' Names on Ballot? N: No Y: Yes	Are Electors Bound? N: No Y: Yes YP: Yes, with penalty
Alabama	PO	N	Y
Alaska	PO	N	Y
Arizona	CO	Y	N
Arkansas	CN	N	N
California	1	N	Y
Colorado	PO	N	Y
Connecticut	CN	N	Y
Delaware	CN	N	N
District of Columbia	CO	N	Y
Florida	CO	N	Y
Georgia	CN	N	N
Hawaii	CN	N	Y
Idaho	CN	Y	N
Illinois	CN	N	N
Indiana	CN	N	N

State	Candidates for Elector Are Nominated by PO: Party option CN: Party convention CO: Party committee	Are Electors' Names on Ballot? N: No Y: Yes	Are Electors Bound? N: No Y: Yes YP: Yes, with penalty
Iowa	CN	N	N
Kansas	PO	Y	N
Kentucky	PO	N	N
Louisiana	PO	N	N
Maine	CN	N	Y
Maryland	CN	N	Y
Massachusetts	CO	N	Y
Michigan	CN	N	N
Minnesota	CN	N	N
Mississippi	CN	N	Y
Missouri	PO	N	N
Montana	PO	N	N
Nebraska	CN	N	Y
Nevada	CN	N	Y
New Hampshire	CN	N	N
New Jersey	CO	N	N
New Mexico	CN	N	YP
New York	CO	N	N
North Carolina	CN	N	YP
North Dakota	CN	Y	N
Ohio	CN	N	Y
Oklahoma	CN	Y	YP
Oregon	PO	N	Y
Pennsylvania	[1]	N	N
Rhode Island	CN	N	N

(Table continues)

State	Candidates for Elector Are Nominated by PO: Party option CN: Party convention CO: Party committee	Are Electors' Names on Ballot? N: No Y: Yes	Are Electors Bound? N: No Y: Yes YP: Yes, with penalty
South Carolina	CO	N	YP
South Dakota	CN	Y	N
Tennessee	PO	Y	Y
Texas	PO	N	N
Utah	CN	N	Y
Vermont	CN	N	N
Virginia	CN	Y	N
Washington	PO	N	YP
West Virginia	CN	N	N
Wisconsin	[1]	N	Y
Wyoming	CN	N	Y

1. See "How the States Nominate and Bind Their Electors" in chapter 2 for explanation of the procedures in these states.

1825 Precedents

The following rules, reprinted from Hinds's *Precedents of the House of Representatives*, were adopted by the House in 1825 for use in deciding the choice of a president, when, as then, the choice devolved upon the House.

1. In the event of its appearing, on opening all the certificates, and counting the votes given by the electors of the several States for President, that no person has a majority of the votes of the whole number of electors appointed, the same shall be entered on the Journals of this House.

2. The roll of the House shall then be called by States; and, on its appearing that a Member or Members from two-thirds of the States are present, the House shall immediately proceed, by ballot, to choose a President from the persons having the highest numbers, not exceeding three, on the list of those voted for as President; and, in case neither of those persons shall receive the votes of a majority of all the States on the first ballot, the House shall continue to ballot for a President, without interruption by other business, until a President be chosen.

3. The doors of the Hall shall be closed during the balloting, except against the Members of the Senate, stenographers, and the officers of the House.

4. From the commencement of the balloting until an election is made no proposition to adjourn shall be received, unless on the motion of one State, seconded by another State, and the question shall be decided by States. The same rule shall be observed in regard to any motion to change the usual hour for the meeting of the House.

5. In balloting the following mode shall be observed, to wit:

The Representatives of each State shall be arranged and seated together, beginning with the seats at the right hand of the Speaker's chair, with the Members from the State of Maine; thence, proceeding with the Members from the States, in the order the States are usually named for receiving petitions, around the Hall of the House, until all are seated.

A ballot box shall be provided for each State.

The Representatives of each State shall, in the first instance, ballot among themselves, in order to ascertain the vote of their State; and they may, if necessary, appoint tellers of their ballots.

After the vote of each State is ascertained, duplicates thereof shall be made out; and in case any one of the persons from whom the choice is to be made shall receive a majority of the votes given, on any one balloting by the Representatives of a State, the name of that person shall be written on each of the duplicates; and in case the votes so given shall be divided so that neither of said persons shall have a majority of the whole number of votes given by such State, on any one balloting, then the word "divided" shall be written on each duplicate.

After the delegation from each State shall have ascertained the vote of their State, the Clerk shall name the States in the order they are usually named for receiving petitions; and as the name of each is called the Sergeant-at-Arms shall present to the delegation of each two ballot boxes, in each of which shall be deposited, by some Representative of the State, one of the duplicates made as aforesaid of the vote of said State, in the presence and subject to the examination of all the Members from said State then present; and where there is more than one Representative from a State, the duplicates shall not both be deposited by the same person.

When the votes of the States are thus all taken in, the Sergeant-at-Arms shall carry one of said ballot boxes to one table and the other to a separate and distinct table.

One person from each State represented in the balloting shall be appointed by the Representatives to tell off said ballots; but, in case the Representatives fail to appoint a teller, the Speaker shall appoint.

The said tellers shall divide themselves into two sets, as nearly equal in number as can be, and one of the said sets of tellers shall proceed to count the votes in one of said boxes, and the other set the votes in the other box.

When the votes are counted by the different sets of tellers, the result shall be reported to the House; and if the reports agree, the same shall be accepted as the true votes of the States; but if the reports disagree, the States shall proceed, in the same manner as before, to a new ballot.

6. All questions arising after the balloting commences, requiring the decision of the House, which shall be decided by the House, voting per capita, to be incidental to the power of choosing a President, shall be decided by States without debate; and in case of an equal division of the votes of States, the question shall be lost.

7. When either of the persons from whom the choice is to be made shall have received a majority of all the States, the Speaker shall declare the same, and that that person is elected President of the United States.

8. The result shall be immediately communicated to the Senate by message, and a committee of three persons shall be appointed to inform the President of the United States and the President-elect of said election.

Party Rules

Charter and Bylaws of the Democratic Party, Article III, Section 1

The Democratic National Committee shall have general responsibility for the affairs of the Democratic Party between National Conventions, subject to the provisions of this Charter and to the resolutions or other actions of the National Convention. This responsibility shall include: . . . filling vacancies in the nominations for the office of President and Vice President. . . .

Rule 27 of the Republican Party Filling Vacancies in Nominations

(a) The Republican National Committee is hereby authorized and empowered to fill any and all vacancies which may occur by reason of death, declination, or otherwise in the office of Republican candidate for President of the United States or Republican candidate for Vice President of the United States, as nominated by the national convention, or the Republican National Committee may reconvene the national convention for the purpose of filling any such vacancies.

(b) In voting under this rule, the Republican National Committee members representing any state shall be entitled to cast the same number of votes as said state was entitled to cast in the national convention.

(c) In the event that the members of the Republican National Committee from any state shall not be in agreement in the casting of votes hereunder, the votes of such state shall be divided equally, including fractional votes, among the members of the Republican National Committee present or voting by proxy.

(d) No candidate shall be chosen to fill any such vacancy except upon receiving a majority of the votes entitled to be cast in the election.

Allocation of Electoral Votes among the States, 1992–2000

State	Number of Electoral Votes	State	Number of Electoral Votes
Alabama	9	Louisiana	9
Alaska	3	Maine	4
Arizona	8		
Arkansas	6	Maryland	10
California	54	Massachusetts	12
		Michigan	18
Colorado	8	Minnesota	10
Connecticut	8	Mississippi	7
Delaware	3	Missouri	11
District of Columbia	3		
Florida	25	Montana	3
		Nebraska	5
Georgia	13	Nevada	4
Hawaii	4	New Hampshire	4
Idaho	4	New Jersey	15
Illinois	22		
Indiana	12	New Mexico	5
		New York	33
Iowa	7	North Carolina	14
Kansas	6	North Dakota	3
Kentucky	8	Ohio	21

State	Number of Electoral Votes	State	Number of Electoral Votes
Oklahoma	8	Utah	5
Oregon	7	Vermont	3
Pennsylvania	23		
Rhode Island	4	Virginia	13
South Carolina	8	Washington	11
		West Virginia	5
South Dakota	3	Wisconsin	11
Tennessee	11	Wyoming	3
Texas	32	Total	538

SOURCE: Norman J. Ornstein, Thomas E. Mann, and Michael J. Malbin, *Vital Statistics on Congress, 1991–1992* (Washington, D.C.: Congressional Quarterly, 1991), table 1–1 ("Apportionment of Congressional Seats by Region and State, 1910–1990"), pp. 6–7. To reach the number of electoral votes, we have, of course, increased the number of House seats to which each state is entitled by two.

Notes to Part One

Chapter 1: Introduction

1. *Congressional Quarterly Almanac, 1957* (Washington, D.C.: Congressional Quarterly Inc., 1957), p. 43.

Chapter 2: How Are Electors Appointed?

2. In Maine, each of the two congressional districts chooses one elector and two are elected at large; this means that the state's four electoral votes will be cast for one candidate or three will be cast for one candidate and one for another candidate. In Nebraska, each of the three congressional districts chooses one elector, and two are elected at large.

3. The case, McPherson v. Blacker, 146 U.S. 1; 13 S. Ct. 3 (1892), dealt with the various methods of choosing electors that the states so far had adopted. On state authority respecting the methods of choosing presidential electors, see also Burroughs v. United States, 290 U.S. 534, 544; 54 S. Ct. 287, 289 (1934). On congressional authority to regulate voting in presidential elections—if there are presidential elections—see, for example, Oregon v. Mitchell, 400 U.S. 112; 91 S. Ct. 260 (1970), and Williams v. Rhodes, 393 U.S. 23; 89 S. Ct. 5 (1968). Only Justice William O. Douglas has cast doubt on the unrestricted authority of the states to determine how electors shall be chosen. Speaking for himself alone in Williams v. Rhodes (393 U.S. at 38; 89 S. Ct. at 14), he said: "It is unnecessary in this case to decide . . . whether states may select [electors] through appointment rather than by popular vote, or whether there is a constitutional right to vote for them."

4. Ray v. Blair, 343 U.S. 214 (1952).

Chapter 4: How Are the Electoral Votes Counted?

5. The president of the Senate is, of course, vice president of the United States, and it sometimes happens that he is required to supervise the counting of electoral votes and to announce the results of an election in which he was himself a candidate. Both Richard Nixon (January 6, 1961) and Walter Mondale (January 6, 1981) announced their own defeats, one for the presidency and

the other for the vice presidency. The last president of the Senate to be in the happy position of announcing himself to be president-elect was Martin Van Buren in 1837.

6. John G. Nicolay and John Hay, eds., *Complete Works of Abraham Lincoln* (New York: Lamb Publishing Co., 1905), vol. 11, pp. 8–9.

CHAPTER 6: WHAT IF NO ONE HAS BEEN CHOSEN BY INAUGURATION DAY?

7. Presidents must be natural-born citizens of at least thirty-five years of age and have lived in the United States for at least fourteen years.

Notes to Part Two

CHAPTER 10: THE ELECTORAL COLLEGE AND THE AMERICAN IDEA OF DEMOCRACY

1. *Electing the President: A Report of the Commission on Electoral College Reform* (Chicago: American Bar Association, 1967), p. 3.

2. *Federalist* No. 49.

3. See *The Records of the Federal Convention of 1787*, ed. Max Farrand (New Haven: Yale University Press, 1966), vol. 1, pp. 68–69, 80; and vol. 2, pp. 29–31, 56–57, and 111.

4. The "confederalists" won a temporary and partial victory at the Convention when the express provision for popular election of the electors was barely defeated. (Ibid., vol. 2, p. 404.) The Constitution finally provided that electors be elected "in such manner" as the state legislatures might decide. During the first three elections, electors were typically chosen by the state legislatures. By 1824, in all but six of the then twenty-four states, electors were being popularly elected. Ever since 1832, popular election has been the universal rule with negligible exceptions.

5. For example, see James Wilson's explanation of the electoral device to the Pennsylvania ratifying convention. (Ibid., vol. 3, p. 167.)

6. See remarks of Madison and Oliver Ellsworth (Ibid., vol. 2, p. 111).

7. Ibid., vol. 2, p. 57.

8. Alexander Bickel wisely stressed the importance of the Electoral College to federalism in *Reform and Continuity: The Electoral College, the Convention, and the Party System* (New York: Harper Colophon Books, 1971). See also excellent discussions in Judith Best, *The Case against the Direct Election of the President: A Defense of the Electoral College* (Ithaca: Cornell University Press, 1975), pp. 119 ff. and 133 ff.; and in Wallace S. Sayre and Judith H. Parris, *Voting for President: The Electoral College in the American Political System* (Washington, D.C.: Brookings Institution, 1970), pp. 51 ff.

9. *Electing the President*, p. 37.

10. In February 1974, although the Conservatives led Labour in the popular vote by 1 percentage point, Labour won three seats more than the Conservatives and was thereby enabled to form the government. See *Britain at the Polls: The Parliamentary Elections of 1974*, ed. Howard R. Penniman (Washington, D.C.: American Enterprise Institute, 1975), p. 243.

11. Since 1900, control of the House has gone four times (1910, 1916, 1938, 1942) to the party that lost the national popular vote. And, counting only the seats contested in any given election, the party that lost the national popular vote won the majority of Senate seats four times (1914, 1918, 1922, 1940) since the passage of the Sixteenth (direct popular election) Amendment in 1913.

12. For an astute discussion of the way such mathematical masochism "abstracts from political realities," see Judith Best, *The Case against Direct Election of the President*, pp. 78 ff.

13. Not everything can be dealt with here, but a footnote excursion on one more staple charge against the Electoral College as undemocratic is irresistible. This concerns the alleged disenfranchisement of those who vote for the loser in each state; their votes are "wasted" because they drop out at the state level from further national calculations. Or even worse, as Senator Thomas Hart Benton long ago complained, popular votes for the loser are in effect added to those of the winner, because he gets the state's whole electoral vote. Those who are horrified by this may take some comfort in one interesting fact. Although such disenfrancisement does indeed occur in every state in every election, it has had absolutely no significance since 1888. A moment's reflection should make this clear. The disenfranchised who vote for the ultimate electoral winner in states where he loses have no complaint; their candidate wins anyway. But how about the disenfranchised who vote for the ultimate electoral loser in states where he loses? Would it make any difference if their votes, instead of dropping out of further calculation, were added to their candidate's national popular vote total, and if popular votes de-

termined the election? The answer is obvious: only when their candidate, although the electoral vote loser, happens to be the popular vote winner. And that has not happened since 1888. Like the popular-vote–electoral-vote discrepancy, of which it is a rhetorically resonant echo, the disenfranchisement problem has been absolutely immaterial for nearly a century.

14. One of the three remaining charges—that the Electoral College mode of electing the president is "indirect"—we may pass over. The ABA Report does not make much of the charge; and what it makes of it, we have already dealt with in discussing the status of the electors as originally intended and the federal mode of counting the presidential vote.

15. See chapter 18 of Hobbes's *Leviathan* (Oxford: The Clarendon Press, 1909), p. 141.

16. The last seriously disputed presidential result occurred after the Hayes-Tilden election of 1876. And even then, the dispute had nothing to do with any defects in the electoral system, but rather resulted from irrepressible conflicts in the tragic aftermath of the Civil War.

17. There have only been about ten of these (the exact number is in doubt) out of about twenty thousand electoral ballots cast—a tiny handful, hardly even a statistical trace. And never once has a "faithless" ballot been cast with the intention of influencing the outcome of an election. They have all been cast for symbolic purposes only, and, ironically enough, usually as a symbolic response to majority opinion in the aberrant elector's home constituency. In short, it is about as likely that "faithless electors" will usurp an election as it is that the English Crown will reassume the regal power of, say, Henry VIII. Neither likelihood seems great enough to warrant the constitutional transformation of either system.

18. See Nelson W. Polsby, *Political Promises* (New York: Oxford University Press, 1974), p. 161.

> The temptation under a direct election system would be strong for all manner of demagogues and statesmen— whoever can raise the money—to run, whether sectional candidates or movie idols with widely scattered following, to appeal directly to the people. So there would be a high probability that under the [direct election plan] . . . the run-off would be the true election, and the initial election would look a bit like the start of the Boston Marathon with its motley crowd of contestants.

Notes to Part Three

APPENDIX A: PROVISIONS IN THE CONSTITUTION FOR PRESIDENTIAL SELECTION

1. This text of the Constitution is taken from *The Constitution of the United States of America: Analysis and Interpretation*, Senate Document no. 92–82, 92d Congress, 2d session, 1973. This document does, however, contain an obvious (and serious) error: The word "member" appeared in the original. We have substituted the correct word, "number." It should also be noted that in this document the term Vice President is sometimes hyphenated and sometimes not.

2. The part included in square brackets has been superseded by section 3 of the Twentieth Amendment.

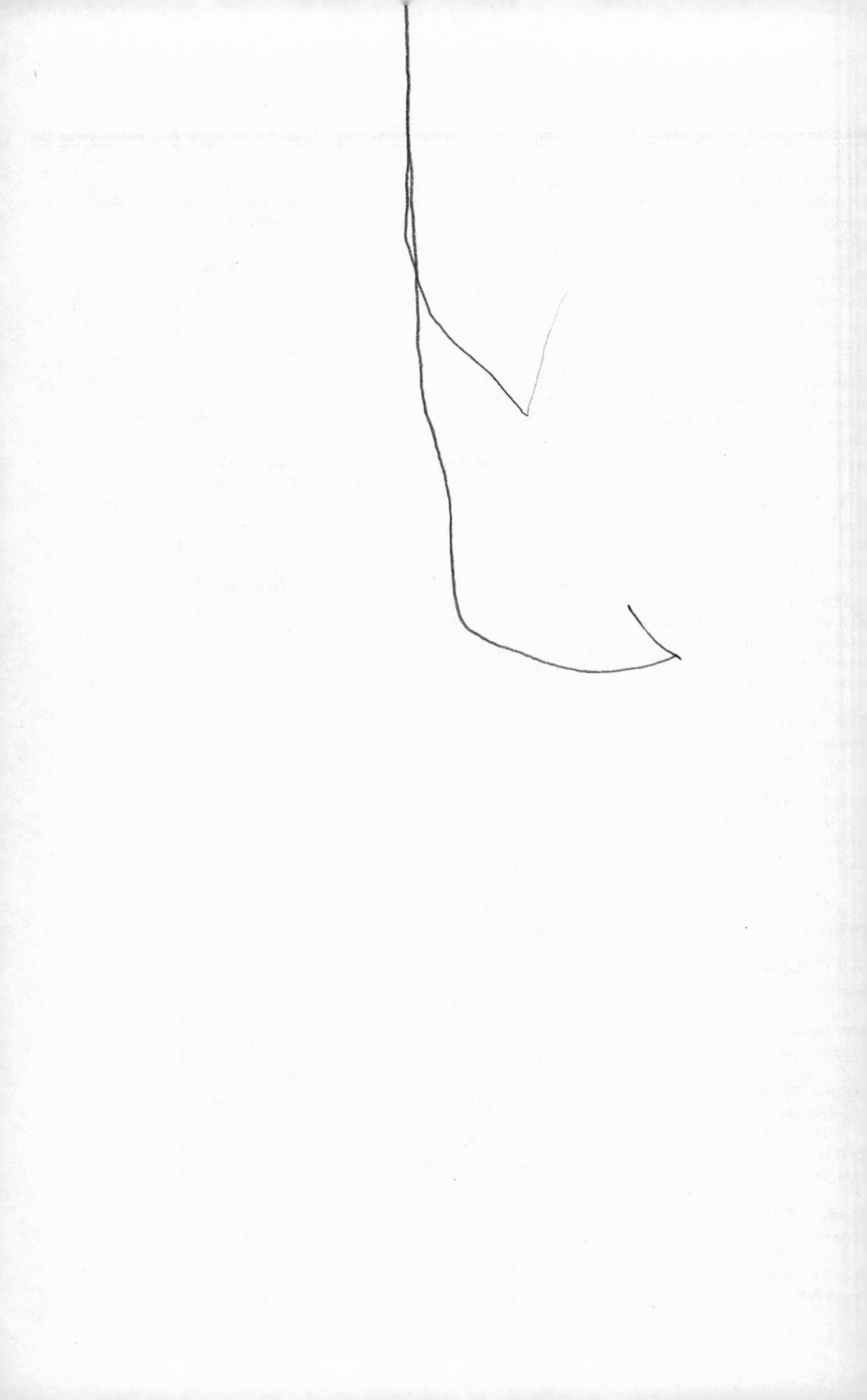

A NOTE ON THE BOOK

This book was edited
by the publications staff
of the American Enterprise Institute.
The text was set in Palatino,
a typeface designed by
the twentieth-century Swiss designer Hermann Zapf.
P&M Typesetting, Inc., of Waterbury, Connecticut,
set the type, and Edwards Brothers Incorporated,
of Ann Arbor, Michigan,
printed and bound the book,
using permanent acid-free paper.

The AEI PRESS is the publisher for the American Enterprise Institute for Public Policy Research, 1150 17th Street, N.W., Washington, D.C. 20036: *Christopher C. DeMuth*, publisher; *Edward Styles*, director; *Dana Lane*, assistant director; *Ann Petty*, editor; *Cheryl Weissman*, editor; *Susan Moran*, editorial assistant (rights and permissions). Books published by the AEI PRESS are distributed by arrangement with the University Press of America, 4720 Boston Way, Lanham, Md. 20706.